Praise for ROAR

"The founding fathers thought it best that women not vote. The founding fathers never met a woman like Scottie Nell Hughes. As you turn the last page of her first book, *ROAR*, you'll feel much more confident that America's female voting population could well become the bloc that finally turns the tide back toward liberty, self reliance, and pride in America."

Neal Boortz, Former talk radio host and author of
Maybe I Should Shut Up and Go Away and *The FairTax Book*

"In an era of a bogus 'war on women,' Scottie Nell Hughes offers a powerful antidote of truth. *ROAR* is a courageous political manifesto and a deeply personal story. Most importantly, it is a passionate call to action for women who care about the future of America. We have more power than we think. As Scottie argues, now is the time to use it."

Monica Crowley, Ph.D., Fox News analyst and
nationally syndicated radio host of *The Monica Crowley Show*

"America has its modern-day superwoman—Scottie Nell Hughes. As a mother of two she's head chef, homework checker, and person in charge of fun. As a private citizen she's the protector of the Constitution, main street, and freedom. A purveyor of grassroots passion in all forms of media from radio to television to the Internet, her distinctive voice rings loud and clear. Some might even say it *ROARS*. It should make us all sleep easier knowing that Scottie, armed with Christian values and unparalleled determination, is always fighting for truth, justice, and the American way."

Charles Payne, Fox Business Network and
founder & CEO of Wall Street Strategies

"Scottie Nell Hughes is the original Steel Magnolia! She has that rare combination of southern charm and big city street smarts. It's quite a thing to watch her take on liberals as she confounds them with her clever commentary. You must read *ROAR*! Her inaugural book is like a cold glass of sweet tea on a hot summer day—it'll quench your thirst and your soul! In my book, Scottie Nell Hughes is one classy lady!"

Todd Starnes, Radio host, Fox News contributor,
and columnist for HumanEvents.com and TownHall.com

"*ROAR* should be read by every woman in this country. Scottie Nell Hughes speaks from the heart and tells it like it is. Scottie stands up for conservative principles and pushes back against the mainstream media's idea of the modern woman. The book is both refreshing and interesting."

Michelle Fields, Political reporter and commentator
and regular contributor to Fox News

"*ROAR* is a brilliant read! This book is packed with common sense and intelligent solutions to an array of issues that America faces today. As a conservative woman, it is refreshing to read Scottie's perspective on issues we care about most. *ROAR* is a must-read for every American patriot!"

Amber Barno, Writer, frequent *Hannity* guest,
Concerned Veterans for American spokeswoman,
and former U.S. Army Kiowa Warrior helicopter pilot

"Scottie Nell Hughes is a wonderful mix of beauty, brains, and Southern sass. At a time when the conservative woman is under attack from all sides, but quietly lauded across America, *ROAR* is just the megaphone that's needed to speak over the stereotypes and initiate tough conversations about the important issues we face every day. Scottie will not be silenced—I encourage everyone to hear her *ROAR*!"

Laura Keehner Rigas, Vice president of Wise Public Affairs
and former communications director for CPAC

"Scottie Nell Hughes has it all. She's worked hard, but also lived and loved. Scottie speaks from the heart, and with her Southern charm and no-nonsense tough love she shares her observations about women today and why we shouldn't let mainstream media suck us into shunning traditional roles. Scottie practices what she preaches and proves that women today who are strong and ambitious in the workforce are also loving and compassionate partners and mothers. In *ROAR*, Scottie will motivate you to not only reevaluate the tremendous challenges facing women and our country today, but to do something about it."

Lori Rothman, Fox Business Network

"Scottie brings a unique combination to the roundtable of political debate. Her experiences as a suburban mom and wife, combined with her passion for her country's future, is a breath of fresh air. I wish we had 10 million more women like Scottie Hughes."

Paul Stanley, Political opinion editor for *The Christian Post*

"Scottie Nell Hughes is one of the most popular guests on my show, with listeners always asking when we're going to have her on again. She addresses the issues head on as only she can—with her intelligence, Southern charm, and bold beliefs. Anything Scottie writes is a must-read for today's conservatives."

Sara Marie Brenner, Host of *The Sara Marie Brenner Show*

"As critics try to put the Tea Party in a casket and women peer out at the landscape of the 2016 elections and declare their role, this Tea Party mother roars her way out, leaving them all pale and aghast! There's poetry in that! It is time for the patriotic woman to *ROAR!*"

Dr. Gina Loudon, Host of *Smart Life with Dr. Gina,*
World Net Daily

"From our first meeting on the ground in Iraq during the peak of the war, through her time as a behind-the-scenes radio producer, to her on-camera triumphs, and now as author of this groundbreaking book, I have watched Scottie Nell Hughes prove herself time and time and time again. Because of Scottie's unique sense of humor, her tenacity, her intelligence, and her leadership in the Tea Party Movement, I'm sure this book is only the first of many important, must-read works to comes from her. *ROAR* is for anyone who wants to understand the truth about conservative women and join the strong movement Scottie represents."

Rusty Humphries, Weekly columnist, blogger, and
daily video-show host for *The Washington Times*

"A Tea Party mom who clearly knows the Tea Party is far from dead emphatically makes her case in *ROAR!*"

Ann Marie Murrell, Founder of Politichicks

"The first time I met Scottie Hughes, she was in complete command of a room full of conservatives. She's a dynamo, she's a leader of men, and conservatives need to read *ROAR* to find out what she knows."

John Hawkins, President of Right Wing News

"When I joined this conservative movement, Scottie was there showing me the ropes and gave me great guidance. I love her to death, and with every bit of help she's given me, one thing is for sure . . . she's taught me to *ROAR*!!!"

Wayne Dupree, CEO, Founder of NewsNinja

"The liberal mainstream media seems obsessed with a make-believe conservative war on women. The reality is, there is a war, but it is by liberals against conservative women. Fortunately, we have great conservative women like Scottie Nell Hughes who are standing up and speaking out. *ROAR* is part of that call to arms to reject big government solutions and embrace freedom."

Sal Russo, President and Founder of The Tea Party Express

"God did us all a favor when he put a Y Chromosome next to two XXs and unleashed Scottie Nell Hughes on American politics. Asking her a question about the issues that confront the country she loves is like taking a shot of stiff whisky—it wakes you up, sharpens your focus, and brings tears to your eyes. Believe me, every time she's on the radio with me, I only need to ask the first question and then sit back and smile. In *ROAR*, she makes the case for the values of conservatism, refutes the Democrat Party's "war on women," and offers up some of the best ideas for making America live up to Reagan's 'Shining city on a hill.'"

Lars Larson, Host of the *Lars Larson Show*

"Scottie's voice is not special because she is a woman. She just happens to be a woman. Foremost, she is a patriot. A passionate, proud, committed, effective patriot."

Michael Berry, The Czar of Talk Radio

ROAR

The New
Conservative
Woman
Speaks Out

Scottie Nell Hughes

WORTHY
PUBLISHING

Library of Congress Control Number: 2014940725

ISBN: 978-1-61795-376-7 (hardcover w/ jacket)

Cover Design: Studio Gearbox
Cover Image: Barry Morgenstein Photography
Interior Design and Typesetting: Christopher D. Hudson & Associates, Inc.

Printed in the United States of America
14 15 16 17 18 LBM 8 7 6 5 4 3 2 1

Contents

CHAPTER ONE

Why We Need to Find Our ROAR

EDIT ARTICLE. CHANGE out washer to dryer. Add dry clothes to pile in corner of room for folding. Check Tesla stock . . . don't need to sell. Restart frozen computer. Let dogs out. Confirm Fox News hits next week. Try to book hotel reservations. Fix peanut butter pancakes and cereal for breakfast. Call next hotel because first price will never get approved by Kellen. Load dishwasher. Clean up dog poop upstairs. Have interview with Orlando radio station on Obamacare. Holler at kids to pick up bonus room or else they don't get playdates tomorrow. Oh wait . . . I need to schedule playdates for tomorrow.

Fix second helping of peanut butter pancakes for Lexi. Send Facebook messages to moms for playdates. Give dog thyroid medicine. Send article to TPNN, Townhall, and Christian Post. Let dogs back in. Confirm conference call with publicist to talk about book cover. Tweeze eyebrows. Order baseball team hats for Saturday (pay overnight shipping fee). Receive breaking news alert on phone . . . Yikes! Send quick tweet about breaking news.

Call Mom and Dad and find out how the funeral went. (Yes, I know my cousin is skinny and her kids are perfect. Why didn't I get those genes? I don't know. Can we move on?) Remind Chris to switch money from "fun account" over to primary bank account so I can pay half of Verizon bill hoping they won't shut off phone. Break up screaming match and . . . "No, Lexi, you cannot sell your brother!" Send e-mail to Ted Cruz's press secretary, confirming interview next week. Brush teeth. Tell kids to brush teeth (which doesn't mean they will). Yikes! Whose video is that on my website? Send note to get it removed. Take vitamins. Send donation letter to baseball team parents . . .

AND IT'S ONLY 10 A.M.!!

More than likely you can relate to this type of schedule and agree that life gets pretty chaotic for us women sometimes. What can I say . . . maybe misery does love company?

I have to turn in two chapters to my book editor in four days, and between now and then my daughter, Lexi, is turning six. My son, Houston, has his first spring game and baseball jamboree, and I need to prepare a Sunday school lesson, host my ninety-one- and seventy-two-year-old cousins for dinner, and get prepped and ready for my NYC trip next Wednesday.

Not to mention the never-ending mountain of clothes that I swear are back in the dirty pile as soon as I move them to the clean pile.

I don't want to belittle my single sisters who I imagine sitting in a quiet room to gather their thoughts and write their literary masterpieces, as I know they have demands of their own. I must admit, at this moment I am green with envy as I imagine a woman sitting curled up in flannels in front of the fireplace with a cup of tea or coffee and her laptop. She is effortlessly typing away as the peaceful snow swirls outside her window. This calm environment can only produce a work full of complete, uninterrupted thought and wisdom.

I don't know why I thought writing this first book was going to be a romantic and blissful experience. I feel like once again I was fooled by some movie that gave me an unrealistic idea about being an author, just as I was when it came to my first pregnancy.

I know I am not the only one who thought her first pregnancy would be filled with cute overalls, afternoon naps in the breeze, and midnight cravings of chocolate-chip ice cream and pickles. The kind of pregnancy where the girl looks "glowing" and her figure with her "baby bump" looks like she is the silhouette on a baby-shower invite.

My first pregnancy looked more like an infomercial for birth control. After gaining sixty-four pounds, I was completely convinced my body was being cruelly controlled by an ex-boyfriend who wanted to inflict as much pain on me as I did on him. The only blissful moment was when I could finally soak in a tub at the end of a day. But alas, that too would be ruined when I later looked in the mirror at my pale, discolored, zit-covered skin and formerly blond, now naturally mousy-brown, frizzy hair and wondered how God could ever put a woman through this transformation and call it a blessing.

Writing this first book is exactly like being pregnant with my first child: *torture*. But despite all of the pain, I look at this miracle known as my child and I would go through all of the suffering again because I know I produced a person who someday will make a difference in the world.

Despite the stress and the lack of sleep this book has caused me over the past few months, the message within needs to be told. I have to speak out so that other Conservative women will know they are not alone in their quest to save their family, their communities, and their country.

Today's Conservative woman does not get to be made from a cookie cutter, as we are all coming from different backgrounds, environments, situations, and viewpoints. Many of us today were blessed to be born with a voice and grow up in an environment that encouraged us to grow in opinion and expression. Yet, because of the ever-changing dynamic of today's society and the aggressive assault of the Progressive agenda, I believe many women today are realizing the power of their emotion and their voice within their own microcosm.

Thanks to social media, every woman has the same opportunity to influence another in regard to all subjects under the sun, including fashion, health, and child raising. Therefore, we need to realize the strength we have as individual Conservative women to make a difference and, when united, to tap into our collective, unlimited potential to fight those on the Left. Regardless of whether you have one hundred or one thousand followers on Twitter or enough friends on Facebook to fill an auditorium, those are potential voters, and they are going to either choose to vote alongside your values or vote to take them away.

THANKS TO SOCIAL MEDIA, every woman has the same opportunity to influence another in regard to all subjects under the sun, including fashion, health, and child raising.

Lies from the Left

There is no subject or area in our time that has been left alone by the Left. Nothing is sacred to them, and to most people who fall left of the center line, regardless of what they call themselves, the ultimate goal is to take control from your hands and put it into the hands of those who agree with their point of view. This is not only a redistribution of wealth; rather, this is a redistribution of life. From their point of view, they are the good and we Conservatives are the bad.

The weakest link in the Conservative movement today unfortunately falls on the shoulders of the female. So many in our movement have decided to stay quiet for various reasons or simply because we are overcommitted. But notice the superficial story told by the Democrats that Conservative women are ignorant, Kool-Aid-drinking fools who are unable to make our own decisions without the guidance of our fathers, husbands, or other male influencers.

This type of twisted thinking couldn't be further from the truth as today's Conservative woman is not one who can be so easily defined and stereotyped. Yet, why is it that the Left can so easily create a PR campaign that sells the false, slanderous narrative about today's Conservative female? When I think of strong female leaders, the majority of the most obvious ones who come to mind are on our side. Those women on the Left who have taken the spokesperson role are not as numerous, and yet the overall perception is that the majority of women today fall into this political persuasion.

Let's take the most prominent leading lady of the Left, which is undeniably Hillary Clinton. Ask any self-identifying Democrat, female or male, who the most prominent heroine is and Hillary Clinton would be their quick response. In a 2014 *Washington Post* poll, the former First Lady found herself dominating 6–1 over her nearest contender, Vice President Joe Biden, for the coveted place at the top of the 2016 ticket for the Democrats. The only other woman on the list of possible nominees for the presidential nomination on the Democratic ticket was Elizabeth Warren, who was only a few percentage points behind the VP.[1]

Sprinkle in Wendy Davis of Texas, former Speaker of the House Nancy Pelosi, MSNBC host Rachel Maddow, and a few outspoken yet outdated Hollywood celebrities, and the list of Democratic ladies is few.

On the reverse, however, are the ladies of the Republican party. Names like Michelle Malkin, Sarah Palin, Ann Coulter, Laura Ingraham, Michele Bachmann, Megyn Kelly, and S. E. Cupp are easily recognized . . . and this is just the tip of the iceberg. I cannot Google "Republican female leaders" and create enough filters that will produce less than one hundred thousand entries, each bearing names I consider to be recognizable by those on both sides of the aisle.

Some might say the only reason I am more familiar with names of ladies within my own party is that we are usually more familiar with our own side, so to be truly fair and balanced I decided to call one of my outspoken Democrat friends and ask her opinion about some of the leading ladies on the Democratic side.

Enter a friend of mine who has grown up in politics, with her father elected to serve in local office for many years of her life. She and I share pretty much the same social circles, same place in life, and at one point even the same Sunday school class. However, we find ourselves on opposite sides of the political spectrum. She and I have a mutual respect for each other and our political beliefs, and rather than focusing on the obvious differences, any political discussion we have either ends in finding a source of common ground or we just don't agree. I value her honesty, and while I strongly disagree with many of her stances on social issues, her insight into the justification allows me to realize where the weaknesses exist on both sides of the argument. Her answers did not surprise me; however, they did confirm one of my suspicions: Republican women like to see other Republican women use their voices to gain the spotlight on issues. Democratic women would rather see the issue be in the spotlight based on its own merits.

For some reason, those in the Conservative movement—but especially Conservative females—don't like to stand alone. We like to know that we have somebody on our left and somebody on our right fighting and saying the same thing we are. We are emboldened even further when we see a female highlighting issues and stating her opinion on the national scene. We can see the arrows the Left is going to throw and then predict how the intensity of the attack will be on our own stage.

It appears that whenever Conservative women actively protest a decision that goes against their principles and values, they will more than likely—and quickly—become a target for assault by the Left, both personally as well as through mainstream-media mockery. Our movement as a whole is a very respectful movement, and finding the right balance of pushing the issue while not disturbing the innocent is extremely difficult.

WHENEVER CONSERVATIVE WOMEN actively protest a decision that goes against their principles and values, they will more than likely—and quickly—become a target for assault by the Left, both personally as well as through mainstream-media mockery.

Identity Crisis

We are the movement of nice. The severity of our protest goes to the extent of tying up traffic within a five-mile radius of a Chick-fil-A or crashing a cable network's website because we sent e-mails in support of Grandpa Phil. We don't riot or burn symbols of our nation in protest. In fact, most of our rallies look more like large church gatherings where you wear either a collared shirt or a patriotic T-shirt.

Overwhelmingly, I believe it is safe to say Conservatives believe in a safety-in-numbers strategy. However, the problem is that the Left is not afraid to stand alone and proclaim their opinion. They are not afraid to get in your face and scream, because their movement is not a movement based on respect and, more importantly, longevity. The more obnoxious the commotion they make and the chaos that follows, the higher in rank the instigator is lifted. However, a Liberal's life in the public spotlight is often short-lived.

This is why Democratic women who rise to be recognized as household names are rare. They are encouraged to act with extreme behavior, and once they draw attention to the topic, they fade into the background. The media can then label the *person* as crazy but not the *movement*. The topic and the Progressive angle are now in the spotlight for as long as the mainstream media thinks it can spin it to demonize those on the Right. There is no better example of this than antiwar activist Cindy Sheehan, whose son was killed by enemy action in the Iraq War. Her protests were constantly the topic of the evening news in 2005 as she created a makeshift camp outside President George W. Bush's Texas ranch.

While most antiwar protests across the country were peaceful and sprinkled with small examples of craziness, almost every action or word spoken by Sheehan was truly done as a shameless PR stunt. In August 2005, Sheehan demanded a second meeting with President Bush, but when it was refused she told members of Veterans for Peace, "I'm gonna say, 'And you tell me, what the noble cause is that my son died for.' And if he even starts to say freedom and democracy, I'm gonna say, 'Bull—. You tell me the truth. You tell me that my son died for oil. You tell me that my son died to make your friends rich . . . You tell me that, you don't tell me my son died for freedom and democracy.'"[2] She also vowed not to pay her federal income tax for 2004 because that was the year her son was killed.

Cindy Sheehan continued her screaming and rants; however, after her antiwar message was brought to the forefront of most political discussions because of her four-week campout, her name disappeared from the news almost as quickly as it emerged. Over the next few years very little attention was given to Sheehan's congressional run against Nancy Pelosi, the IRS suing her for tax evasion, her various arrests outside of key government buildings like the White House and the UN, and even her current bid for governor of California barely gained a headline or even attention from a Left-wing newspaper editor. The mainstream media and the Democrats were done with Cindy, as any further attention to her would only expose the idiocy of those within their movement.

On the other hand, very rarely do you find a Republican spokeswoman on an issue disappear once her topic has passed the news cycle. Sarah Palin is a great example of this. Palin became a household name almost overnight when she was selected as Senator John McCain's running mate in 2008. However, after their defeat, the former governor of Alaska has continued to be at the front of most controversial issues, usually representing the most conservative viewpoint on that topic. Headlining many Conservative conferences, about to release her fourth bestseller, and signed for a second contract as a Fox News contributor, former Governor Palin is probably the most recognized name of all the Conservative women, and she is far from being ready to fade into the sunset.

Why, then, do Democrats continually get to label themselves the party for women if they so quickly bury the majority of their own? Even history shows that women should primarily find themselves deep in the trenches of the Republican Party. The founding mothers of the women's movement—Susan B. Anthony and Elizabeth Cady Stanton—were Republicans, and the first suffragettes were seated as delegates in 1870 at the Massachusetts Republican State Convention.

Up until the 92nd Congress (1971–73), women elected to Congress were fairly balanced between both parties. The status quo was kept for fifty years until this time when the distribution went from six Democratic female representatives to five Republican female representatives, to eleven Democratic to four Republican female representatives. Since then only twice in the early eighties have Republican women been able to outnumber their Democratic counterparts, and today we are outnumbered seventy-six to twenty-three. Ouch![3]

If numbers alone were the reason why the Democrats were allowed to claim the title of the party for women then I would never lose sleep as numbers can always change. The problem is, the Democrats have a monopoly on the emotions involved in politics. They have done a spectacular job of defining the issues that women should care about and, more importantly, deciding what positions a woman should take on those issues.

Issues like the economy, education, entitlements, and health care are usually universally important to every American regardless of gender; however, every demographic is going to have issues that might directly impact them. For those within the black community, equality and race discrimination are important; Hispanics are largely focused on immigration reform. The homosexual community looks for marriage equality laws. Women are no different.

Very rarely do I like to reference radical feminist writers; however, over one hundred years ago Emma Goldman, in her essay "The Tragedy of Woman's Emancipation," wrote about four issues that are still as prevalent in today's society but have been manipulated by the Left to guarantee there will never be any solution.

Goldman points out the following:

1. Men dominate many of the most esteemed professional fields—and get paid more for their work.
2. Work stress disproportionately impacts women.
3. The "freedom" the workplace supposedly offers a woman sometimes doesn't feel so free at all.
4. Women are doubling up on work at home and outside of the home.

While I agree these issues are just as prevalent for today's woman, today's Liberals continue to use these issues as excuses to create crutches for the victim to hobble on. This is no surprise, considering the concept of enabling the victim to help create more victims is the entire foundation of the Democratic party. Those within the party claim they are more sympathetic and only want to help. However, the reality is the Democratic party uses entitlements and government programs to enslave its followers and guarantee its own survival based on the use of taxpayer funds to buy votes in the ballot box. The amazing part is that those chained to the system are completely fooled into thinking they are free. The dollars they receive from the government are not an earned paycheck but money they are entitled to because they are the victim of some injustice done by American society.

The Conservative woman, however, sees these same timeless obstacles and takes a more pragmatic approach, saying, "It is what it is." She doesn't whine or cry and she immediately starts working on a solution to get over it. We don't sit and focus on the problem; rather, as Conservative women, we start to focus on a solution. We are active, which means while our Democratic counterparts are finding ways to use their tears to appeal to female masses, we are too busy trying to eliminate the issue all together.

WE DON'T SIT and focus on the problem; rather, as Conservative women, we start to focus on a solution.

The problem is, many of these issues are never meant to have a solution as the rules of nature are outside human control. Maybe in the future, some mad scientist will be able to develop a way to allow men to birth babies, and then we can all be on equal footing. However, I would have to question the sanity of a culture that encourages such technology. Men are from Mars and women are from Venus, right? There are emotional, physical, and social differences between the opposite sexes. Conservative women accept this and respect the differences while it seems our Liberal counterparts acknowledge but lament these differences, continuing their "woe is me," victim-themed message. I refuse to accept such an insulting point of view that tells me I am inferior to men since they are dominating me both in the workplace and home.

Role Models

The Republican viewpoint on gender roles should be much more appealing to women because we respect our differences and we know that we are not comparing apples to apples. Rather, our comparisons are of two different products and while the results might be the same, that doesn't mean one is better than the other. The Conservative viewpoint actually encourages women to identify, grow, and utilize their talents rather than to just give up and become victims.

This is why I think many Conservative women don't ever want to play the role of the victim, knowing that it's a role you will never be able to give back. I don't know if I would call it pride; *respect* seems more appropriate. I have been blessed to grow up in a very Conservative community where Conservative women seem to grow as strong as our magnolia trees. Don't get me wrong, the area has produced fine modern-day Republican patriarchs like Fred Thompson, Bill Frist Jr., and the late Howard Baker; however, ladies like Congresswoman Marsha Blackburn and Congresswoman Diane Black were not just thrown onto the national scene. Rather, they grew as representatives of their local communities and then the state before being sent to DC. These women were, in both cases, strongly supported by the other Republican women in the area. It is well known by candidates for office that if they have not acquired the support of the local Federation of Republican Women, they should not put down a deposit for a victory celebration because the actions of these women can make or break any Republican campaign.

In my own life, it was these women whom I watched, beginning at an early age, as my mother always had me involved in either the church or the local political group. Whether I was nine years old and standing out in front of the Nashville Planned Parenthood holding a sign asking people to please stop abortions (not understanding the full meaning of the many curse words I heard being thrown at me from the cars driving by) or fighting a school rezoning issue that was going to remove me from my local high school, my mother made sure I was constantly surrounded by both men and women who showed that there was more to the term *voice* than just the words coming out of one's mouth.

The ladies who taught me the value of my opinion and the best way to utilize it were those Republican Women of Williamson County. Those women would put any skull-and-bones, underground shadow group to shame, except they fearlessly did all of their work in the sunlight while wearing their grandmothers' pearls and carrying their concealed weapons in their designer purses. I watched this group of women rally behind candidates who believed in protecting the taxpayer and preserving our constitutional rights as American citizens, and rarely did I not see them celebrate alongside them on victory night. These women would welcome a new member and within one meeting assess her talent and utilize it for the cause. Whether it was making centerpieces for a fund-raiser, putting together yard-sign frames, or baking loaves of bread to feed campaign volunteers, they considered no job or detail more important than another, and in the end they all celebrated the victory together. I bet you can think of a similar group of women in your own life . . . women who worked together regardless of age, background, or economic status, all with the same ultimate motivation.

These women came from various backgrounds but were united behind the motivation to elect Republicans to office, from the city alderman all the way to DC. Not only did they accomplish their goal for their own county—as no Democrat would even dream of running for office in Williamson County—but because their energy was contagious, they passed along their formula to the other Republican women across the state. I truly believe the reason why the state house, senate, governor, both senators, seven out of nine congressmen, and the majority of municipal leaderships in the Volunteer State are red is because of the women of the state of Tennessee.

The funny thing is, in most cases the number one reason why women are afraid to speak out is honestly because of other women. It is our nature to want to be loved even if it's just by one other person. But I believe the majority of us want to be loved by everyone. More often we hear the term "people pleaser" applied to a woman than to a man. It is our natural tendency to want to have friends and be included most of the time in a group. Our insecurities are our own worst enemy. Whether you're an introvert or an extrovert, a loner or a socialite, every woman has her own comfort zone, which is built on the approval and acceptance of not only herself but of others.

I'm not saying this is wrong, but this is just how it is. Many women today don't want to speak out about their personal political beliefs for fear they might be ostracized by a group or a friend. The problem is, most people take this silence as either meaning they agree with what is being said, they don't care about what is being said, or they don't know anything about the topic being discussed.

The political ideology you believe in generally speaks to how you handle and interpret silence. Silence is not golden in many cases, as the absence of words can be easily misinterpreted. While those on the Right use silence to show respect with hopes of not escalating the conflict by inserting dissenting viewpoints, the Left views silence as a sign of agreement.

This is very dangerous and one of the main reasons why I think the lies of Liberal women can be easily sold. So we on the Right either have to do a better job in making sure *silence* is not perceived as agreement . . . or, better yet, we need to learn to speak out when something is being said that goes against our beliefs.

Now, some women might project the attitude that they really just don't care—that sticks and stones may break their bones but names will never hurt them—but I find it hard to believe that even the strongest women like the late Margaret Thatcher, Dr. Condoleezza Rice, and even Ann Coulter have not privately broken down into tears over something that was said or something that was written. Many might see tears and crying as a sign of weakness; however, I see them as signs of honest compassion and humanity knowing that they are not so hardened by life that they are unaffected by words.

Words are extremely powerful, and the more we care about or respect someone the more their words and opinions affect us. It's sort of like public speaking. I get much more nervous when speaking in front of an audience who knows me and whom I have to face after the speech is over. My fear of disappointing or offending those near and dear to me often causes unnecessary anxiety. I would much rather speak in front of a group of strangers, knowing that if I mess up, stumble, or embarrass myself in some way (knowing it might end up on YouTube), sympathy will come from those closest to me without the awkwardness of being live in the same room.

The reality is, at some point even the most intelligent person says something stupid. The most graceful will trip and the most confident will have a bad day that makes them cry at the most insignificant comment. As Conservative women, we must all learn to live by a version of the Golden Rule. We must treat others within the movement as we ourselves wish to be treated. And when those in office representing us do something well, we should praise them as enthusiastically as we attack them for doing poorly.

Right now we have a great opportunity to correct the inaccurate message that says the only place for today's women is on the left side of the aisle. Not since the suffragette movement has the issue of women in politics been center stage. Those within the Democratic party have done this with a well-coordinated strategy of demonizing and shaming those of us women on the Right into thinking that we were either alone in our opinion or there was no place for it within the Republican party.

WE HAVE A great opportunity to correct the inaccurate message that says the only place for today's women is on the left side of the aisle. Not since the suffragette movement has the issue of women in politics been center stage.

It's time we Conservative women begin playing offense instead of defense when it comes to informing the public as to which party sees women not as mannequins of their storefront but as key players in the makeup of their platform and policy for the present and the future.

We need to educate with honesty about the history of American women and our strong Conservative roots instead of regurgitating the biased propaganda of the Left. Most importantly, we need to find ways to encourage other women who might be diverse in their lifestyle, yet who honestly share the same political ideal to seek their own special way to ROAR!

CHAPTER TWO

Blame It on Genetics

ALTHOUGH THIS CHAPTER is light on politics, I think it's important for you to know a little bit about my background so you can better understand who I am and why I do the things I do and say the things I say. I believe every person's life could be made into a Lifetime Original Movie; however, there are definitely parts of mine I feel would be more appropriate on Comedy Central. We know our genetics decides things like the color of our hair, our skin tone, and even our chances of getting a disease. But have you ever considered that maybe your personality can also be mapped back to your gene pool?

Now, it's easy to blame my size-eleven feet and the fact that no matter how much I starve myself I will never see myself in a single-digit clothing size because of my biological father's side.

I trace my thin hair and big bosom straight back to my mother's side. But is it fair for me to say that my outgoing, ambitious, loudmouth self is also outside of my own control? That I am genetically programmed to push myself until everyone is happy and that my attraction to politics was predetermined?

In reality, it's a miracle that any of us are here on this earth today. Truly, only one small decision at any point of time could have changed the course of events that made our birth possible. Did you ever wonder how you got here? I am not questioning the big picture of evolution versus creationism, because while I have met some men I swear descended from apes, there is no doubt in my mind that the only way I got here was because God created not only me but every generation before me.

What is very peculiar is that up until recently, I didn't know exactly where I came from. However, the gaps that have been filled explain so much that I now know the strength I thought I developed on my own was actually already built into my DNA. Now, I can't go back too far, but what I do know makes me look weak compared to the challenges that the women in my bloodline overcame.

This is the story of how I got here . . . or so I have been told, as some ghosts and graves in one's life never need to be dug up. However, this is the story I have pieced together.

A Hard-Working Heritage

The year 1929 challenged America and all of her people. It was the beginning of the Great Depression. The economy was devastated and it would stay that way until WWII began. It was during this decade that two young farm girls, my grandmother and her sister, left their family in Southern Illinois, boarded a train, and went three hundred miles north to Chicago looking for work. My grandmother, Nellie Treece, was fourteen years old and her sister, Eve, was fifteen.

These two young girls had a goal: to get jobs so they could buy for their parents the forty-acre farm that they were currently living on as tenants. That determination and strength of will came from their mother, Nora, a diminutive woman who kept her family going by selling the asparagus she grew, the eggs her chickens produced, and the butter she churned after milking her cows.

Nora, a devout Christian, would take her little brood across the fields every Sunday morning—regardless of rain, snow, or sunshine—to the church she helped found and build. She made sure each child was taught the Bible and was baptized when they received Christ as their Savior. She met her children's physical and spiritual needs and took her mothering responsibilities as seriously as she took her church and community responsibilities. She was an activist.

When Nellie and Eve stepped out of the train at the Illinois Central Railroad Station they were scared, but they never lost sight of their goal and quickly made Chicago their new home. Finding a room in Mrs. Collins's boarding house was the young girls' first accomplishment. Fortunately Mrs.

Collins became a protector to the girls. She helped them learn their way around the city as they went looking for jobs.

Within a week of job hunting, both Nellie and Eve were hired by Aldens—also known as Chicago Mail Order Company—to work in the shipping department. They each were paid thirty-three dollars a week. (In contrast, their last job before leaving home was picking strawberries for fifty cents a day!) Despite their healthy pay raise, frugality remained a way of life for them. Within two years, these young teenage girls took the train home with enough money in their purses to purchase a house and farm for their family. The two sisters had accomplished their goal and were now free to move out of their little room in the boarding house and get a small apartment on Chicago's West Side.

Nellie and Eve continued to work at Aldens, with my grandmother quitting work when she got married at the age of twenty-seven. Nellie was a strikingly beautiful, fiercely independent woman. She was known to advise others to never tell a man you love him, as he will take advantage of you. After her death, this was verified by my grandfather, who said in thirty years of marriage, she never said "I love you" to him. He, on the other hand, adored her—even though they were like oil and water together. She was the typical frugal, Depression-era woman, while he was like a character out of a Damon Runyon novel— bigger than life and one who spent money from his many endeavors with great relish. It would take a woman of strong commitment to be married to a man like my grandfather.

He was heavily involved in Illinois politics. As a lobbyist, he kept a suite of rooms at the Democratic headquarters at the St. Nicholas Hotel in the state capital of Springfield. There were two political arenas in Illinois during my grandfather's time: Dick Daley's Chicago and Paul Powell's Downstate Southern Illinois. Each area had its bosses and ways of conducting business. My grandfather's influence was mainly in Downstate Illinois, but he also worked in Mayor Daley's territory.

To keep his wife busy, freeing him to come and go as he pleased, he bought my grandmother a very large, double-entranced apartment building, which had twenty-seven apartments, eight garages, and six parking places, on Chicago's West Side. Nellie stayed happily busy for many years running her apartment buildings. She made a great deal of money and kept her tenants happy while her husband stayed at the state capital for weeks at a time. It was a marriage of two very strong people who found a way to stay out of each other's paths.

My grandmother lived by hard work and independence—two virtues she learned from her mother and passed on to mine. I now realize that hard work and independence are not possible without one key element: strength.

MY GRANDMOTHER LIVED by hard work and independence—two virtues she learned from her mother and passed on to mine. I now realize that hard work and independence are not possible without one key element: strength.

My Mother . . . Myself?

There is possibly nothing more complex or challenging than the relationship between a daughter and her mother. I have found, though, that the older I get, the less judgmental my mother and I are of each other. I now realize and accept that she probably will not change, and she knows that there are some mistakes I am going to have to make and lessons I must learn for myself.

Growing up, I harbored a lot of resentment toward my mother for not being like the rest of the mothers I knew. She didn't play tennis or drive a Suburban. She didn't work, yet that doesn't mean she was a Suzie Homemaker either (she used duct tape to hem all of my clothes). I became angry at her because she didn't seem to have the energy and excitement that other mothers did when it came to bake sales or planning girls' shopping trips. But I didn't know my mother's past. Or the part I did know was sugarcoated to protect me.

My mother grew up in the same apartment bought by my grandfather to keep my grandmother out of his hair. My aunt Eve and her husband Jerry were in the same apartment building, as well as other family members who rotated in and out of the bottom floor at different times. It was a type of communal living, but everyone was related and the responsibility for raising my mother was equally shared by everyone in the building. I imagine my mother was pretty smart as she had been double-promoted in elementary school. She must have also been a handful to raise because at the beginning of her sophomore year, my grandmother granted her request to go to a Catholic boarding school in Springfield, Illinois. Mother, thinking she was going to gain freedom from her very strict family, was unpleasantly surprised to learn the nuns at Sacred Heart Academy were much worse.

In the 1960s, there were not many career paths women were encouraged to study in college. Women at that time were sent to college for two reasons: either to be employed as a nurse or teacher, or the more desirable possibility, to find a husband. My mother, never one to accept society's standards, entered Southern Illinois University as a pre-law student. However, being the impatient one on class registration day, she ended up jumping into the shortest lines semester after semester, which just happened to always be for speech and theatre classes. By her junior year, Mom realized that she was never going to have enough hours to graduate pre-law so she declared education her secondary, and after seven years she finally had enough hours to graduate. But like everything else in her path, graduation was not without drama—and a little help from the National Guard.

At that time, students at SIU and many other colleges across the United States were protesting the Vietnam War. On May 4, 1970, Kent State held a protest, which was invaded by the National Guard and led to an altercation between the soldiers and the students. At the end of the day, guardsmen had fired sixty-seven rounds over a period of thirteen seconds and four students were dead, nine others wounded. Fearing similar violence, SIU students voted to close their campus for the remainder of the spring semester. All students were given a withdrawal pass for their remaining hours so, as fate would have it, my mother graduated without having to finish her most difficult classes, which she had put off till the end.

Having become a teacher now, all she needed to do was find a husband, and she did, marrying the first guy who proposed. A small wedding on the courthouse steps to a nice man named Bob was quickly followed by the birth of their son on the first day of fall in 1967. Life quickly became routine as Mother settled into a life that quickly broke her free spirit.

My grandfather, being deeply involved in the political scene, knew of the growing use of an instrument being used to detect white-collar crime—the polygraph. Knowing my mother's intuitive skills and ability to talk her way out of almost anything, Grandfather knew there was no one better able to see through the lies of criminals than one who knew how to do it so well herself. At his urging, Mother applied to the Backster School of Lie Detection in New York City, where she became the first female not only to enroll but also to graduate and enter the field as a commercial polygraph examiner.

Unfortunately, many of the top partners at security firms she interviewed with would not hire her because they felt a woman would never be welcome in the industry and could not handle the emotion of dealing directly with the worst criminals. However, Bruce Goldstein, a young, rich Jewish man in Minneapolis, saw something in Mother and knew she was just the person he needed for his rapidly growing firm.

This was the beginning of the liberated woman. This was truly the "I am woman, hear me roar" era. Women knew no boundaries and most didn't make excuses or use their gender as a crutch. (The whining of feminists didn't start until the '80s.)

Mother handled hundreds of cases ranging from first-degree murder to high-dollar, intricate corporate theft. She soon became known for her interrogation skills and started teaching interrogation and leading seminars, which landed her the role as director at the Zonn Institute of Polygraph. Unfortunately, while her career was taking off, her personal life was falling apart.

Following her mother passing away and her father falling ill, things became even worse when she and Bob divorced after growing apart because of her increasing professional success and travel schedule. Still, they remained friends because of their five-year-old son, Cliff.

Mother and Bob shared custody of Cliff; however, Mom kept their son as her work moved them from city to city. Too busy to have much of a life outside of work, Mother tried her best to spend as much time with Cliff as possible. This little boy was said to be the mayor of any town he lived in, instantly making friends of all ages. One of my mother's favorite memories of Cliff was his love of calling radio stations and talking to the DJs. So many times, Mother would catch him calling in to chat on various topics. Just recently Cliff's kindergarten teacher told my mother that Cliff was the most social child she ever had during her tenure of teaching.

Making a Family

We don't talk about the first day of spring in 1976. It's been that way for as long as I can remember. That March 20th in Atlanta started off like any other as my eight-year-old brother headed off to school wearing his blue ball cap and backpack. My mom remembers him yelling back into the house, "I love you, Mom!" before shutting the door. That was the last time she saw Cliff. The last time she heard his words. The last time she felt his touch.

To be honest, I didn't know the truth about that day until just recently. My mother had always sheltered me from the story, as no girl wants to grow up thinking that her brother was murdered at a young age. I was always told that Cliff and the nanny's son had been playing cowboys and Indians when the boy had grabbed the rifle from the mantle and, not realizing it was loaded, accidently shot Cliff. The truth was that the nanny's son shot my brother point-blank through the heart.

Day by day my mother somehow continued to breathe. I asked her once about the boy, and she told me that she had written a letter to him, saying she forgave him and hoped he would not continue to live a life of violence. For her own sanity, she had to let go and look to a future where truly very few reminders of her past were left.

My mother threw herself completely into her job. One day, thanks to President Carter visiting Atlanta, Mother chose to enjoy dinner at her secretary's house instead of fighting traffic. It was there that she met another guest at this home—a dark-haired, olive-skinned man of medium height, with deep, sky-blue eyes.

Lloyd Semler was talented in art, music, acting, and modeling. However, he wasn't talented when it came to love. Having been married twice before and having three children, he was definitely what most women considered a free spirit. Both he and my mom were hurting when they met each other, with demons and ghosts that filled their hearts and minds with guilt.

But just because God is your matchmaker doesn't mean the courtship is a breeze (as they quickly found out) so they eventually split up. Mother was doing great professionally while Lloyd continued to struggle in his profession. However, my mother wanted to have another baby, and after trying to get pregnant for months upon months, the stress ultimately broke them apart and Lloyd headed back out on the road. Mom, heartbroken again, found herself fully devoted to her job, where she eventually met Tom, who was tall and successful and . . . married.

Now, I really don't want to think about my mother being anything but fully dressed and baking cookies, but the reality is it was the '70s and she ended up getting pregnant with Tom's baby. Mother was delighted in her pregnancy. But she was lonely and her heart still hurt from the loss of Lloyd. One fateful day, Lloyd called to check in and see how Mom was doing. He, too, had been feeling completely miserable.

"Do you love him?" Lloyd asked Mom upon hearing the news she was pregnant. "Do you love the baby's father?"

"Of course not. I love you," my mother replied.

"Then please let me have the baby with you," Lloyd said. "I will take her as if she was my own and we will create a complete and whole family out of these shattered lives we have lived in the past."

With that, my mother and Lloyd were back together and this time with a baby on the way. And I would have a father. Life was beginning to shine again for Linda Davis.

On June 21, 1980, after a long night of contractions and ice cream and potato chips, I came into this world with the fiery spirit of my mother and immediately grabbed hold of the finger of my blue-eyed daddy. My mother had a family again.

Time for an Update

I'm grateful for the women in my family who have set a great example to follow, and I hope to do the same for my daughter. Although I'm still learning, I believe the key to having a healthy mother/daughter relationship is finding a way to define and respect the role each should play—and the dynamics and roles change as girls become young ladies and mothers become grandmothers. Regardless of the stage in life, though, there will always be moments when the mother is driving the daughter crazy or the daughter is making some choice that the mother disagrees with. Mothers have to realize their daughters' lives are theirs to live, so we must help them grow into the strongest, brightest, wisest women they can be.

Now that I have my own daughter, I can see where it is easier to have a stronger opinion over the choices a daughter makes than those a son makes. I will be the first to say I am not a psychologist, but I know the mistakes I made and the pain they caused, so I justify my sexism toward Lexi because I don't want to see her hurt in the same way. However, I fear the resentment she could potentially feel toward me because she does not understand my reasoning.

This same resentment could also be used today in politics. It seems like today's Republican party is trying to adjust its definition and stance on issues. This could be seen as trying to rebel against the party of our parents. We see this mainly on social issues rather than fiscal. However, just as in life, everything is usually eventually woven together.

How do we as today's new Conservative women rebel against a party whose history is filled with ignorant speeches and quotes on a variety of issues from some of its most notable members? Quotes from our past, such as this one from President Eisenhower with regard to racial segregation after the *Brown v. Board of Education* decision: "These are not bad people. All they are concerned about is to see that their sweet little girls are not required to sit in school alongside some big overgrown Negroes." Or even from a present-day politician such as Todd Akin, who said as he was running for Missouri Senate, "If it's a legitimate rape, the female body has ways to try to shut that whole thing down."

Sure, the Democrats say stupid things every day, but while our comments end up headlining every newscast, they have the power of the mainstream media to help cover their idiocy so their comments never get traction.

To bring it back into relatable domestic terms, it's like we live in a neighborhood where our home is right next door to a snarky, sneaky, creepy neighbor armed with binoculars and video camera at the ready. The kind who will call the home-owners association immediately when our grass gets higher than an inch or when we forgot to wheel the trash can back to the garage by 5 p.m. However, on the other side of this neighbor is a rundown crack house, where a stream of visitors constantly park all over the yard—a concept that would seem impossible considering the tall weeds that look like they would require an industrial tractor to mow. This house is not only left alone by the HOA, they are daily brought meals and given money by the house in the middle.

Therefore, not only as women but also as Conservatives, we have to find a way to update our agenda without compromising the founding principles and morals on which we stand and that make us different from the other side. We cannot completely retreat from our original positions on traditional marriage, abortion, entitlements, and immigration in order to make us look more attractive or "compassionate."

Just like our past and our genetics have a large impact on the persons we are today, the same can be said about the Republican party. Our past is what caused our creation and our stance on issues is what made us the dominant party in the past. The trick is, we need to find a way to dispel this new politically correct definition of "compassion" that the Democrats have created—a definition that is impossible for the Republicans to ever be able to grasp unless we reduce our moral and ethical foundation and become an almost mirrored reflection of the Democratic party.

I believe this is where some people calling for a third party comes from—frustrated Republicans who only see the lines between the parties being blurred and our foundational strengths being compromised. With the continued introduction of a moderate candidate at the top of the GOP ticket and their continued losses, what political strategist would continue to suggest this is the path for future success? Hopefully, a soon-to-be-unemployed one.

Today's Republican party, just like an adult daughter, needs to embrace the numerous strengths of the past and be able and willing to identify and update those characteristics that are time sensitive while *never* compromising the overall foundation and framework of the party.

CHAPTER THREE

First Comes Love, Then Comes Marriage

THERE ARE A few things a stereotypical southern male expects of his wife: loyalty, a clean house, the ability to keep the children quiet during the fourth quarter of a football game, and to be talented not only in the bedroom but more importantly in the kitchen. Unfortunately, when my husband married me, loyalty was about all I could promise. As for my capability of keeping the children quiet during a football game, that didn't matter because I was usually screaming louder than they were. And my knack for the kitchen was limited to what frozen dinner was on sale and if I liked the color of the box.

I really blame my lack of culinary skills on my parents, who were both remarkable cooks. I remember many arguments from my parents as to who was cooking that night and what type of bread crumb would taste better in the meatloaf and whether oregano or basil should be the dominant spice in the spaghetti sauce. Needless to say, a diet never lasted too long in my family. Some might think this would be a blessing, and growing up I was thrilled that my dinner table was usually filled with neighbors and guests looking forward to whatever delicious dish either one of my parents cooked. But now that I am responsible for my own dinner menu, I have realized that while I inherited my mother's gift of gab and my father's aptitude for never meeting a stranger, culinary skills are definitely not part of my genetic makeup.

Rewind to the beginning of June a few years ago when, after spending a few hours at the playground with two other domestic divas and hearing of their home-cooked-dinner plans, I felt inspired to go home and fix my own family a dish that would surely give Paula Deen a run for her apron. After spending twenty-five minutes gazing at my pantry trying to figure out what I could make with a can of tuna, some Baked Lay's, and raisins, I decided on a form of tacos, thinking that with enough cheese anything could taste good.

Six hours later at 3:30 a.m., when my hubby and I were sharing a moment over our porcelain toilet, he turned to me, his face a pale shade of green, and politely said, "Honey, I love you . . . but please never cook dinner again!"

Genius. I was a genius! After almost five years of marriage at that time and countless hours of scrubbing burnt skillets or swallowing small bites of food with mouthfuls of sweet tea to hide the taste, I had figured out how to never cook again! Sure, it was a long night and an even longer day; but not only had my hubby and I lost a total of six pounds in a twenty-four-hour period, I would never have to worry about what to fix again! And even better, because my hubby had *asked* me to forgo this duty, I would not have to feel guilty for not cooking again.

Fast forward, where after six weeks not only had my hubby and I gained back the six pounds plus ten more, my children could tell the day of the week by what drive-thru window we were visiting. My mother-in-law the weekend prior had told me when she realized the lack of nutrition in my family's diet, that cooking was like riding a bike and I just needed to get back up after falling off.

Determined to start a new chapter in my cookbook (or maybe just start writing it in the first place) and with the patient help of the aproned recipes lady at Publix, I decided to make my family their first home-cooked meal in over a month. Southern peach baby back ribs, corn on the cob, and balsamic tomatoes were set as the menu for my reentry into the kitchen, and after my mother-in-law's sweet words of encouragement the weekend before I thought it would be best to have her and my father-in-law over for dinner as well. Coincidentally, my husband called in the middle of my cooking to say he was going to miss dinner, and while I contemplated who might have seen me at the grocery store and tipped him off, I realized this was probably for the best. If my dinner didn't turn out so well, at least my hubby and I both would not be sick again. On the other hand when the doorbell rang, and my in-laws bravely marched in, I realized that I was using them as guinea pigs and I had hit a new low when it came to taking advantage of others.

Remarkably, the dinner was pretty good, and when my husband returned home later that evening, seeing that all of his family had no shades of green in their skin tone and were happy, he even asked for the leftovers. While I know that I will never be a champion chef or even have the best casserole at the church potluck, I have learned that there is nothing wrong with following a recipe, especially when you realize you are outside your realm of knowledge . . . and that more cheese does not always solve life's problems. That said, all wives sometimes wish there was more cheese in their marriage.

Happily Ever After

Almost every wife at some point has that moment when she realizes that now she has a man and picking up the dirty towels on the bathroom floor is the least of the negatives she now finds in her prince.

ALMOST EVERY WIFE at some point has that moment when she realizes that now she has a man and picking up the dirty towels on the bathroom floor is the least of the negatives she now finds in her prince.

If anyone doesn't think Hollywood has a powerful reign of influence, just look at the effects movies have on one of the key elements of human nature: *love*.

It is at this point when movies and novels like *Fifty Shades of Grey* and *Twilight* become so attractive to this group of women. While I might not agree with every element of any of these stories, find me a woman in this world who doesn't want to add a little extra sizzle to her marriage . . . a woman who is happy just cleaning pots and pans and doing laundry and organizing the attic and has no desire to be surprised by flowers, to feel treasured and beautiful, or to be swept off her feet by the man of her dreams.

As little girls, we grow up watching all of the princess movies thinking that one day our prince will come. We are swept up into thinking that even a girl plagued by a hardship has the opportunity to be rescued by a man. Up until recently, almost every Disney princess movie had a romance that could only be termed as fantasy. True love is always the end result and guaranteed to produce a couple who live *happily ever after*.

Then as our hormones are racing in our teenage years, the dream of passionate kisses in the middle of the school gym or the moment of being chosen over the more popular, beautiful girl by our crush becomes our dream. The concept of being done wrong by a guy is introduced; however, the situation is always rectified with the bad guy getting what he deserves and the girl landing in the arms of another, cuter option, once again living happily ever after.

Then you move into your single adulthood, and all of a sudden, finding a movie without a wedding or talk of a wedding in it becomes almost as rare as finding a guy who enjoys watching one with the word "romance" in the description. The majority of movies aimed at this demographic of women only continue to encourage the dream that a man will eventually sweep us off our feet and a true-love moment will occur where fireworks and leg pops happen at the first kiss.

Finally, once women realize that Hollywood is not reality and find a way to justify our own reality as a fairy tale, we settle down and get married.

Don't get me wrong. Marriage is great and filled with many rewards. I love the fact that I don't have to worry about a date to an event or a wedding, or that I always have someone whom I can cry in front of and admit my insecurities to. I love having someone who is supportive of my crazy ideas but has also gotten the hang of how to rein in my enthusiasm without hinting about his doubts at my chance of achieving my goal. Finally, I love having someone who knows when I have reached my breaking point even when I fail to admit it. And, whether it be with a simple flower or a carb-filled treat, knows how to bring a smile to my face.

In today's society, especially one influenced by Hollywood, we have done a good job of making women feel like they should completely ignore the ideas of romance, fantasy, and passion. We learn we should just leave that idea for the movie scripts as we are only setting ourselves up for failure, and the earlier we understand that and become cold, the less chance we have of being hurt. In fact, as with anything in life, usually the more we wish for or count on something, the greater the chance of being disappointed. What I find to be interesting is how different types of women handle their guaranteed disappointment.

One of the major arguments that my husband and I always have is that I hold him to these fairy-tale standards and wish for him to plan surprise romantic moments for us. Then when I basically have handed to him the outline of the plans for *exactly* what I want on a silver platter, I get angry at him when he doesn't take it.

I vent about wanting attention and wanting him to surprise me just once with something he has planned from the very beginning to the very end. I plan all of our family trips from the reservations to the packing, but I would like my hubby to take care of every last detail in regards to family vacation, celebration, or an everyday adventure just one time.

I take it personally and get angry when he doesn't do it, thinking that he is selfish or that he just views me as a slave to his house. In reality, I am holding him to standards that are only in my mind because I viewed them in a movie or read them in a book.

We have established that movies and books can influence dramatically the experience of love at all stages of a woman's life. I guarantee they can have the same amount of influence on a variety of other elements in a person's life.

Movies for Women vs. Movies for Men

In 2013, a new study by Vocativ (via Jezebel) showed that movies which passed the Bechdel test actually made more money than those which failed. (This test considers works of fiction that feature at least two female characters focused around a plot that doesn't involve one of the male characters.) *Mama, Oz the Great and Powerful, The Heat, Frozen,* and *The Hunger Games: Catching Fire* were all box office powerhouses that championed strong female characters. All of these movies target different age groups, and the hope would be they would have the same effect of encouraging women to be strong as other movies encourage women to fall in love. The big difference is, while it is hard to find a movie where the end result is a woman not falling in love, not being rescued, or not having the dream passionate kiss, there are plenty of examples in pop culture where the strong female character is either demonized or ostracized, guaranteeing that her life will not be lived happily ever after, regardless of whether there is a man involved.

Why is it that in male-targeted movies, the concept of love is generally just introduced either because a woman might be watching and will quit her complaining about having to watch that film, or so that men can get a glimpse of a young, attractive woman? Please tell me an example of a movie where a male viewer ended up cheering for the strong, dominant woman to win in the end over a man?

Please introduce me to the husband and wife whose introduction, courtship, and marriage was just like a Hollywood screenplay. Some might be like *When Harry Met Sally* while others might be more like *The Notebook*. I'm sure there has to be a couple like this somewhere or else Hollywood has been able to brainwash an entire civilization into believing a completely false narrative.

Bringing the Movies Home

Now, you might say that men are not affected by Hollywood. But truth is, I think many of us women build up resentment toward our significant others because our lives are not like those in the movies we are watching. We get angry and hold our spouses accountable for the absence of romance that more than likely they didn't realize they were responsible for providing.

It's not like most men grew up watching the same movies we did or read the same romance novels we did. So why do I smack my hubby on the arm at a cheesy line being said on TV? Or get the dreamy-eyed look from watching a male character's monologue only to magically turn my gaze to ice when I look at the hubby as if to accusingly say, "You should do that"? I am not really giving him a fair chance, am I? He truly is clueless as to what I am expecting, even after eight years of marriage.

Does this mean I give men a pass for not stepping up to the plate or giving up the "game" they had while we were dating? Of course not. But I realize that many times I create the difficulties and the tensions within my own marriage and after chatting with my circle of friends, I realize I am not alone in my frustrations.

When I ask my girlfriends about the romance in their marriage, usually they just roll their eyes and laugh it off with some version of an "I gave that up years ago" remark. The truth is, though, these women do honestly wish for their hubbies to step up and do something surprising and romantic, and we are not just talking about flowers.

WHEN I ASK my girlfriends about the romance in their marriage, usually they just roll their eyes and laugh it off with some version of an "I gave that up years ago" remark. The truth is, though, these women do honestly wish for their hubbies to step up and do something surprising and romantic.

I remember one day, my husband called me on his way home from a late meeting and asked if I wanted anything. I replied with a simple no followed by, "I have only been taking care of *your* children all day, washing all of *your* clothes, and now I have been standing for the last three hours ironing all of *your* shirts and pants."

He innocently replied, "Okay, I love you and will be home soon." Thinking I had made my point, you can imagine how I felt when he walked in thirty minutes later empty-handed and I had to strongly resist the urge to throw the shirt I was currently ironing onto the floor and stomp on it.

What ensued was a ten-minute lecture during which my husband dared not even blink for fear I might throw the starch can at him. When I finally had run out of air, he responded with a simple, "But I asked, and you said no . . . for goodness sake, I don't speak woman!"

At that point I realized that my husband was not at fault for he was honest in his request and was simply doing what I told him to do.

I once asked a friend how she kept her marriage hot and spicy after eighteen years, and her reply was simply, "I wear sexy underwear to bed."

Excuse me? Really? The answer to all my problems was within the walls of Victoria's Secret? Simply stated, Crystal explained that most men are visual and in many cases motivated by sex. While we women need romance, men desire visual stimulation just as much. Therefore, if I was not providing my husband the ability to see me in a sexual way (the birthday suit only works for so long) by wearing old torn-up boxers and T-shirts to bed, then was it fair for me to expect him to give me what I desired?

While I can say that I did not completely exchange my comfortable pj's collection for lacey outfits that look more like they might fit a doll from my daughter's collection, I do know that if ever I need special attention or romance (or the credit card bill comes in), I have just the trick.

The Political Parallel

Too bad Victoria's Secret didn't have something in its catalogue that would get those elected to office to notice the American people's needs.

In a way, many of the same characteristics we look for in a spouse are what we look for in our political leaders. We as a people want to trust. We want to know our leaders will be loyal, strong protectors of our core beliefs and be willing to defend us against any attacks. We want our politicians to be honest, effective, and good providers. Finally, we look for our politicians to put us, the people, first and above all other professional commitments.

So many times in politics, just as in love, we find politicians come onto the scene riding a beautiful steed, grabbing all of the attention in hopes of securing victory and saving the day. We can easily become infatuated, politically speaking, with the new, fresh politician. However, all too often the voter is let down by their representative. The politician breaks trust, either by a single wrong vote or action, and just like a marriage relationship, once that bond of trust is broken, how hard is it for one to earn it back?

I have the joy of being married to a politician and while he has only served in a local office, I imagine the issues are the same at all levels. All that changes is the level of impact and number of people his decisions affect.

Different Backgrounds

Chris always had a love for history and the political system, so he chose to study history in college. Growing up, we had different approaches to dating and love. Being the typical girl, I was slightly boy crazy with my sights always set on guys out of my league: the class president, the star of the football team, or the guy everyone loved to hang out with. Unfortunately, my overly ambitious "strive for perfection" attitude mixed in with Amazon-woman genetics that made me five feet ten by twelve years old didn't really make me appealing to any of the objects of my affection. By the end of my sophomore year, I just gave up trying to find love within the halls of my high school and decided to date a perfectly delightful guy named Kris, who just happened to be in college . . . thus taking away any pressure to find dates for school dances and Friday nights.

College was about the same except I switched boyfriends after four years and went for another long-term relationship with a fraternity boy from my same hometown. Believe it or not, his name was Jesus, and while our fights were epic, we still lasted through college and only broke up a year after when I realized he was not in the ring-giving frame of mind.

Looking back, I could not be more grateful that he did not fall for my weeping tears mixed in with "but I gave you all of my college life" sobs, because our personalities were too alike. We would have been miserable together. Not to mention that neither of us had skinny genetics and our poor kids would have been the poster children for Michelle Obama's "Move It" campaign.

I joke that both Kris's and Jesus's wives owe me a lot of gratitude for teaching their men how to handle high-maintenance women; however, since neither continued communication after our breakup, it makes me doubt how good I might have been for them. I know I am not alone in thinking this; almost every women has dated at least one guy who they knew that upon breakup was different in a better way than when they first met. I am not saying that women are supposed to change men; rather, men change on their own when they realize what makes women happy. A happy girlfriend is always a lot more fun to have around than a bitter, complaining one.

Chris, on the other hand, grew up a completely different way. Despite being class president in high school and captain of the football, baseball, and wrestling teams, Chris had never had a girlfriend. In fact, he spent most of his Friday nights watching Rush Limbaugh's TV show. I am blessed to be friends with many of the girls he went to high school with, and they always say Chris was that guy in school you didn't want to date because you wouldn't want to lose a friend. He was also truly that guy whose ex you wouldn't want to be because no matter what had happened, you would seem like the bad person because he was just that nice.

So, by the time prom came around, he always had an adventure trying to find a date. It's not as if he didn't want to have a serious relationship; his football coach his senior year asked him what he wanted to be when he grew up, and his only answer was "the best father and husband I can be."

College wasn't too much different as Chris never really found anyone he was interested in. After being alone for a few years, he realized he was just not a casual-dating kind of guy.

Having never been much of a partier and having never drunk alcohol, even when he followed in his brother's footsteps and pledged Kappa Sigma, his no luck with dating continued. To make matters worse, Chris had developed a fear of being rejected and upon learning of this, the fraternity brothers made Chris publicly ask a pledge class of sorority girls to go on a date with him at a mixer. In front of everyone, each girl was told to refuse and give him a reason why.

Being alone was much easier than facing rejection by another girl at this point. Despite his friends trying to play wingman and obvious attempts by girls in college, Chris just never found a reason to waste his time or his money on someone with whom he couldn't foresee a future.

That was the exact opposite of me. By the time I was out of college and free from any relationships, I had a new perspective on dating. I had been tied down for seven years and that had not gotten me anywhere. So I was going to date like a guy. God gave me two hands with ten fingers, and I was going to have a boy for each one of them. This didn't mean I slept with them; rather, this allowed me to not get serious about any of them. None of them thought we were exclusive (I hoped), which allowed me to never worry about my heart being broken or becoming emotionally vulnerable. It was a fun few years and very rarely did you find me crying over a guy. Instead, I could focus on getting started in broadcasting, enjoying the friendships, traveling with my core group of girl-friends, and not worrying about being tied down.

For girls who are reading this and are still single and en-joying the adventure of dating, please know that being in pol-itics can be very attractive to most men. I will be the first to say that most guys were not attracted to me mainly because of my looks; rather, they were thrilled that they could have an intelligent conversation. For those guys who were not in the business of politics, they enjoyed having the option to talk about current events along with other typical date conversa-tions. The ones of whom I was the most leery were those who were in politics themselves, as I know they simply were con-stantly assessing if I would be a perfect fit for the role of a politician's wife.

This was really true in DC, and the more ambitious the guy, the more inflated his ego . . . and the more challenging it was to get through a date. The interesting thing was, the more power a guy had, the less motivated he was to flaunt it. These were usually the guys who made me think twice about my ten-finger rule. But then something would come up that would remind me that I was still not ready to settle down.

It is amazing the difference between the type of guy that we date and the type of guy we end up marrying. As most moth-ers do, mine was never shy of giving her advice on the guys I was dating and who I needed to go after. "Don't marry some guy who is hot, suave, and oozing in romance," she would say. "It's just as easy to fall *out* of love as it is to fall *in* love with a guy like this . . . Marry a guy because he will be a loyal husband and good father. Don't expect to be head over heels with the man you marry; rather, love will develop." I can't say that I will pass this same advice along to my daughter, as I do believe we are capable of finding the complete package and I do wish for my daughter to find a partner she constantly desires and with whom she has fireworks exploding every time their lips meet, but who is also a good man.

But as I have learned with many of my friends and their marriages, the guys we think are perfect can turn into the worst terrors behind closed doors. These are the guys who are really good at deceiving women, and while we expect flaws, it is the small red flags we see in dating that become huge banners once there are rings involved.

Women can be strongly attracted to different characteristics. Some like a guy who is physically attractive, others like a man who has a bank account filled with big numbers, others like a man who oozes power. All of these guys may have great character as well but they have to have one main quality that a woman finds attractive.

Due to my outgoing, dominant personality, I find men who hold power within their own environment to be attractive. As anyone who has ever dated a man of power knows, those who use their instincts for good are rare and those who are just looking to do anything to gain more are just as dangerous as a stick of dynamite.

So after a string of bad relationships in which I had chosen to become more emotionally involved, I found myself alone on Super Bowl Sunday night, angry at myself for not sticking to my ten-finger system. My mother, always wise in her words, said, "Most women have to go through misery in order for their eyes and heart to be open for Mr. Right."

In this case, my mother was right, and the very next day I received a phone call from a girlfriend telling me that her Sunday school teacher had been begging her to introduce me ever since he picked me out of a picture at Christmastime. She warned him I was his exact opposite and tried to convince him to meet one of the other eleven girls in the picture, but alas, he was hooked.

We met for dinner three days later. Six months later we were engaged, and nine months later, we were married on the steps of the Tennessee State Capitol. Two weeks prior to the wedding, we had just finished his primary for county commissioner and were excited about the general election in August.

I swear my friends were making bets at the wedding on how long we would last as most people would never imagine matching my extroverted loud personality with his black-and-white, facts-and-figures, even temperament. However, it's that mix that has given us balance and allowed us to clear the hurdles that life continues to throw at us.

After eight years of marriage, I will admit that I was not truly prepared for the changes that occur beyond just taking a new last name.

Discovering Happiness

Finding the answer to what makes women happy seems like it would be simple as long as you didn't ask a man. However, men continuously look for facts and figures to give the answer as to what makes women happiest. Abraham Lincoln once stated that most people are about as happy as they make up their minds to be, and according to the latest study from Arthur Brooks and the American Enterprise Institute, Conservative women are much happier than our Liberal counterparts.[4]

Think about it . . . if you were a man, who would you rather marry: the sweet, happy, witty Elisabeth Hasselbeck, or the negative, authority-neutering Barbara Boxer? Arthur Brooks wrote in the *New York Times:*

> Many conservatives favor an explanation focusing on lifestyle differences, such as marriage and faith. They note that most conservatives are married; most liberals are not. (The percentages are 53 percent to 33 percent, according to my calculations using data from the 2004 General Social Survey, and almost none of the gap is due to the fact that liberals tend to be younger than conservatives.) Marriage and happiness go together. If two people are demographically the same but one is married and the other is not, the married person will be 18 percentage points more likely to say he or she is very happy than the unmarried person.[5]

A Social Capital Community Benchmark survey says Conservatives who practice a faith outnumber religious Liberals in America nearly four to one. And the link to happiness? You guessed it. Religious participants are nearly twice as likely to say they are very happy about their lives as are secularists (43 percent to 23 percent). This is a given considering that for most people, faith is where we find peace and hope.

Brooks's study basically shows that what makes people happy is stability and balance. Usually the main source for this comes from having faith and a family. This is what conservatism is all about.

Another great point from the study is that people find satisfaction and happiness in working and they like to feel that success comes as a result of what they do. There is an inherent unhappiness that eats at the individual when they consistently rely on someone else or on the government.

I found it to be very interesting that when the government was the third wheel of a relationship, couples were more likely to split, according to a study done by the University of Missouri.[6] Considering that money is one of the top causes of arguments—which eventually can lead to divorce—being reliant on someone else, whether it be the government or your spouse, is an obvious breeding ground for failure.

Marriage is not equal; however, that doesn't mean we don't expect our spouses to contribute. Those who rely on the government are just taking another spouse into their relationship.

I couldn't imagine that a marriage based on Uncle Sam being the main provider would be anything but a disaster.

A Party for the Family

Conservative women are usually very optimistic and positive as they work to preserve and promote a country that they love and believe is full of good people who do good work. Liberal women are often championing or looking for a victim, someone who has been done wrong by their environment, their place or position in life, or their government. While it is always great to look out for those less fortunate, it's also important to emphasize the ideas of self-reliance and self-respect and to give a person a real opportunity to stand on their own. This concept is exactly opposite of the Democratic platform, which is constantly looking for ways to make people reliant on the government.

Conservatives encourage women to be genuinely happy and to show it, while it seems that the Democrats don't like their women to show they are happy because that would mean they are content with their position in life. While we don't live in a perfect world, to Conservative women the glass ceiling is not something we believe has to be broken because, to most of us, it has never existed.

I would be amiss if I didn't point out the political celebrities of each party and their public images. While serious at times, rarely do you see ladies like Sarah Palin, Dana Perino, Michele Bachmann, and Nikki Haley without smiles on their faces. Compare them to Nancy Pelosi, Hillary Clinton, or

Janeane Garofalo, who are caught more often in a snarl or a frown. I keep waiting for the comparison of the two sides to be used in an advertisement for Botox or wrinkle filler.

There are always exceptions on both parties' fronts; however, I think it is important that we point out the role models that young girls have to look up to as women they should want to be like, whether in life or in love. We need to teach our young girls to respect and appreciate the differences between men and women; that each gender is just as important as the other; and that while environments and influences might change, there are still lines of definition which have allowed relationships between the sexes to be successful throughout time.

One of the main reasons why I believe marriage is more difficult in today's world is because we have blurred the roles that husbands, wives, and kids play within the household. Not every household is the same and what works for one household might not work for another. The problems usually arise when couples allow their marriages to be influenced by society's opinions or when politicians decide to get involved.

No one to my knowledge has filed for divorce in court stating politics as the reason for the separation. However, financial disagreements undoubtedly are usually the top reason that leads to divorce in America today. The stress that overwhelms couples when they are in debt, or the purpose and priorities of where their money should be spent, are all factors highly controlled by Congress.

This could be debated, but with a quarter of a household's income being given to the government, the local taxes on consumer goods, and the tax on investments, today's Congress is a lot more in control of one's household budget than most people realize.

So why do the Democrats want to keep raising taxes? Do they think they help Americans by taking more of our money? If money issues are already the leading reason why almost half of all marriages end in divorce, could we say that those in Congress are helping marriages fail?

This is a bit of a stretch but another reason why it just makes more sense for women—especially if they are married or hope to be one day—to vote Conservative. Trust me ladies, falling in love is harder than it looks in the movies, and staying in love is even harder.

In the end, I believe this is where the Democratic women are ruining their own future both in love and in life. They view the battle of the sexes as competition and strive to be the "better" sex, while we Conservative women just strive to be equal. Their theory will never advance a woman in the workplace and more importantly, when applied to marriage, will more than likely land them in the conference room of a divorce attorney. Marriage is not 50/50, and anyone who goes into it with that mindset is only setting themselves up for failure. Marriage is a partnership that equals 100 percent all of the time. If you don't have the flexibility, understanding, or patience to constantly change the ratio of give and take with a person, then it looks like you were duped by Hollywood's perception of love.

The question you need to ask yourself when you go into the voter booth next time is the same one you did when you accepted any first date: *Which politician could I be happy spending the rest of my life with?*

CHAPTER FOUR

Parenting and the Mommy Mafia

Dearly beloved, we are gathered here today at our guest bathroom toilet to wish Mr. Fish well on his last swim to the betta fish ponds in heaven. While he was only with us one year, it was a good year filled with two different fish tanks and a variety of multicolored rocks. Mr. Fish kept us company at night and watched us play during the day. He will be missed.

W<small>HY AM</small> I writing a eulogy for Mr. Fish, you might wonder? Don't I have a basket of laundry to put away, dinner to start, or a better way to spend my children's rare naptime than writing words for a dead fish? *Guilt.* I am overwhelmed with guilt. My simple act of kindness and trying to make things better ended up with the death of my son's first pet.

Why is this always the story of motherhood? Try to make things better but most times things only get worse. Take your average dinner night this past holiday season at anyone's house. You're trying to make it through one last meal on the leftover turkey from the refrigerator. Granted, you have already turned it into a casserole, a stew, barbecue, and a potpie, but hopefully your family will not notice it if you add some noodles and cover it with lots of cheese. In my home, the end result looks pretty; however, with the first bite both kids (and my husband) declare, "No more turkey!" and settle on a bowl of cereal. Too exhausted from being creative, I don't protest too much and end up sharing the turkey a la cheese with the dog.

Back to the aforementioned guilt. The guilt eats away at me because my son does not even know that Mr. Fish is dead; rather, he is convinced that Mr. Fish is only taking a nap. On discovering Mr. Fish's lifeless body on the bottom of the tank, he trustingly looks at me and pronounces, "Mommy, Mr. Fish is just sleepy after you gave him a bath yesterday." Great. Now if he realizes Mr. Fish is dead, he will draw the connection that getting a bath by Mommy means later being flushed down the toilet! At that point, it might have been advisable to have gone to the store and bought a new Mr. Fish stand-in, but instead I chose to write a eulogy and have a solemn but tearful ceremony at the commode with my heartbroken son sobbing and asking why God needed Mr. Fish in heaven, didn't he have enough fish? It made me rethink that "honesty is the best policy" thing. Did this scar my son's psyche? Will he have mother issues someday that will be dumped on his wife? Will it ruin his marriage? Will he grow up to be an atheist? Who knows? All I know is I tried to do the right thing and only time will tell if my son will ever forgive me for killing Mr. Fish.

Mommies Rule

One night the following week, still fresh from the Mr. Fish crisis, I was nursing Lexi Lynn, who was suffering with a stomach bug for the third time. I kept myself awake in between medicine doses by flipping through the endless numbers of cable channels. I finally landed on my favorite show, the classic Godfather trilogy. As always in the past, I was hooked. After thirty minutes, I realized how Mafia life was not too far off from what being a suburban mother and wife was like. The group of mothers I ran with operated with as much finesse and stealth as the mob. Granted, our bloodshed usually results from falling off the monkey bars, and our ammunition is Neosporin and *Toy Story* Band-Aids. However, there are many other similarities between the characters of these classic Italian families and the families I interact with every day. That's how I realized that even in my own small hometown we have our own version of a mafia—a mommy mafia to be exact!

According to *Webster's Dictionary*, the term *mafia* does have two negative crime-related definitions, which I happily skipped over. The third definition states that a "mafia" is a group of people of similar interests or backgrounds prominent in a particular field or enterprise. That sure fit the group of mothers I was involved with. Children were our life and we protected our home territory at all costs.

Almost every mother who is actively involved with her child is part of a mommy mafia whether you realize it or not. Your family is not identified by your last name; rather it's by the letters that adorn your vehicle. School name, kids' sports teams, or neighborhood historical societies are just a few stickers that help distinguish where you spend most of your time and money. While women might socialize outside of their "family," it is safe to say most of their friendships are kept within these circles, as it is rare for a member of the mommy mafia to have time to cultivate any companionship outside of her children's circle of activities.

If you're looking to find one of these mommy mafia group meetings, it's not too difficult. On pretty days, simply go to any local park and you will find an organized group of woman with sack lunches in monogrammed lunch bags and matching strollers taking over the picnic benches. Any of the sports fields during their season definitely have a large count of mommy mafia members present; however, beware of the team mom: she is usually the most ambitious of all the mommy mafia members, trying to make sure the postgame snack has the perfect balance of nutrition and kid appeal.

When there are no kids around, mommy mafia members are still hard at work and can be found at Publix or Target, organizing a consignment sale for church or school, or at the local gym trying to work off the last ten pounds from the month they let it all hang out. Yes, we all have those months, but the mafia mothers don't let it get out of hand as you will get some gentle advice from the members along the lines of, "Looks like you need to cut out the chips and do celery for a while." Celery is far easier to face than the mafia members' all-seeing eyes.

While I cannot promise that members will always look like perfection, mommy mafia members can rock yoga pants during the week and be ready to go out for an elegant dinner with the mister on Friday.

I wouldn't suggest messing with any member of the mommy mafia, as their first priority is family! These women are extremely loyal and protective and most assuredly beautiful, but anyone who even has a hint of danger about them will be quickly run off by the mommy mafia and their perfectly manicured nails. These women are warriors.

I WOULDN'T SUGGEST messing with any member of the mommy mafia, as their first priority is family! These women are extremely loyal and protective and most assuredly beautiful, but anyone who even has a hint of danger about them will be quickly run off.

I have watched these women in their dark sunglasses stare down suspicious-looking drivers, giving them the universal "I see you" sign so intimidating that even if the driver was just trying to find a place to eat lunch, they would likely change plans quickly to avoid confrontation with a member of the mafia. I've seen mothers stand out in the road and flag down speeders who were zooming through their neighborhood. These same mothers have successfully lobbied and put pressure on elected officials to give money to needed programs in the school system. Technologies like Facebook, Twitter, and texting have only empowered these women to be able to protect the ones they love even more by quickly spreading the word of injustice and a call to action to their networks.

I wonder if the First Lady would consider herself as part of the mommy mafia. Every opportunity possible during the campaign season, the First Family was constantly on parade. While we knew better, it was a smart move to try and show that even the Obamas suffered some of the same bumps that the average American family does. It made for good politics. However, the disconnect this president has from today's family makes me wonder how much of the Gap shopping is just for show and do the Obamas deal with the same problems as everyday Americans—many of which the president and his wife helped to create. Do you think the rising cost of beef and coffee prices really affect the First Family? I doubt it, but it certainly affects my family and that's why I have a shout out to *all* mob members to protect their territory, including the grocery store, by getting politically informed and active to fight this administration's war on the economy.

Family on the Front Lines

Speaking of war, there is a battle going on today to destroy the traditional American family. As in any war, you must know your enemy and you must have battle tactics with strategies. There are so many spheres of influence on our children, parents today have to juggle. Throughout time, parents have always had challenges; however, what makes the present more difficult is that today's issues are highly visible and complex due to the technologically advanced world in which we live.

In today's parenting world, we are being told constantly by the government what is best for our children and how we should raise them. The government today has even gone a step further in many areas and mandated their suggestions be final, thus eliminating even the choice.

Most of the time, this is done in the name of safety and while helpful, some laws today are overreaching and should be left up to the parent.

A great example of this was that just recently, famed Conservative writer and trendsetter Michelle Malkin's eighth-grade daughter was sent home with a warning letter from the BMI police. The obesity report card lectured Michelle and her husband saying their daughter's body mass index was "very low" and they "should make certain" she "eats a healthy diet that includes the appropriate number of calories."

First, newsflash to any school systems (including my own): if you have a watchdog's child in your system, just know that any example of the nanny state that might occur more than likely will end up in the national news. Second, whether it's too high a count or too low, how dare any government official send home a note telling me whether or not my child is eating healthily. My challenge would be, unless you mighty bureaucrats are willing to come personally to cook a pyramid meal in my home every night and, more importantly, force my children (and husband) to eat it, then don't even begin to criticize. I am lucky if my children's fickle taste buds allow them something other than mac and cheese, peanut butter and jelly, or pizza.

How much a child weighs is not an issue of "national security" as our own Mike Huckabee defines it. Rather, this is just another opportunity for our government to use our children to increase its own reach, budget, and control.

Seat-belt laws are another area that the government has overstepped its boundaries. Do I think buckling in is important? Absolutely. Do I like the thought of my children being strapped down and unable to jump around the car while I am driving? Of course. However, do I think it's right for the government to keep generalizing and mandating that I must keep my baby turned facing backward until they are one year old, or that at seven years old, seventy pounds, and forty-two inches tall, my child must still sit in a booster seat until he is nine? Absolutely not.

If we as Conservatives preach personal responsibility and accountability in every other area of our lives, don't you think parenting should be the same? A parent should have the choice as to what is best for their own child based on their own research, their pediatrician's recommendation, and what the government suggests. The key is, however, that it should not be illegal if my decisions are against what the government says I should be doing.

IF WE AS Conservatives preach personal responsibility and accountability in every other area of our lives, don't you think parenting should be the same? A parent should have the choice as to what is best for their own child.

This is a great example of where the government has taken away the responsibility of choice. Instead of building a generation of educated parents who know more than just what is needed, we have parents who look to the government for all instructions.

There are bad parents in this world, people you wouldn't trust leaving your cat with. The idea that the children of this type of irresponsible parent don't have a chance at a quality life comes to mind. Child-safety laws might give that child a fighting chance of survival but all these children are seeing are their parents doing the bare minimum when it comes to providing a nurturing, safe environment in which to grow up. Therefore, this type of irresponsible parent more than likely creates kids who will follow in their parents' footsteps . . . an endless cycle of parents who just mindlessly go along with orders. Perfect for the mindless voters Democrats need to keep their policies and politicians intact.

This has not always been the case, at least not according to the sitcoms I run across on Nick at Nite. Every once in a while, as I am scrolling through the television channels, trying to go from Fox to CNN, I come across a black-and-white sitcom from the '60s. Whether it is *Lassie, Leave It to Beaver,* or *The Andy Griffith Show,* as an adult viewer I see a common thread that runs through most of the early sitcoms. Most of these shows are family-oriented. The family is the core of the unfolding story. The matriarch of the show fills her day staying at home worried about her dinner and wearing her cute ruffled apron while the man of the show marches off to work in a freshly pressed suit or uniform. The children are usually busy with some conflict that seems trivial in our day and age . . . a boy crying over being picked last for kickball or a girl sad because someone looked at her crossways at school.

Most present-day sitcoms could not be further from the shows of our past. The common thread of family life is still present, but the family has sure changed. The plot usually features kids telling their parents they are gay, pregnant, or joining a gang. The main characters are usually never short of snide remarks and the adults are often portrayed as ignorant figures of authority. Parents are demeaned and shown as clueless people who almost seem worthy of the disrespectful remarks made to and about them. Not to mention, in many sitcoms today husbands and fathers are shown to make idiotic decisions or be the main problem in the family. Parents never hold the juveniles accountable for their rude behavior and comments, and to underscore this dark humor, canned laughter is introduced to emphasize all of the inappropriate dialogue. What a great disrespect of authority figures today's sitcoms reinforce in impressionable children.

Trouble in the Classroom

Besides fighting the media influence in our children's lives, today's parents are in a constant state of confusion with regard to their children's education. Parents don't know whether they are welcome by the school to bring cupcakes for birthdays for fear they will be accused of encouraging obesity, whether they may host a classroom Christmas party, or if a kid may wear a T-shirt with an American flag on it.

In February 2014, the 9th US Circuit Court made it official that a display of the American flag could be banned in a school (including wearing it) if a large enough group of students, teachers, or both threatened violence and the will to do anything about it was not available. The case was brought on by a high school in Morgan Hill, California, where in response to the Cinco De Mayo holiday, several students were threatened when rumors circulated that they were planning on wearing the American flag to school on that day. While this could be termed as a silent protest, the principal, instead of choosing to punish the students who threatened violence, chose to punish the flag-wearing students by sending them home from school. The court stood by the principal's decision, setting the standard that bullies do get their way as long as it is in the name of being politically correct.

Our children's textbooks are filled with math we don't understand. New methods of addition, subtraction, multiplication, and division are being introduced by the Common Core math program that are completely foreign to the traditional math taught in schools in the past. Social studies and history books push to make our children global citizens by downplaying American history and patriotism. This was never better illustrated than when President Obama stated that there is no such thing as American exceptionalism. Common Core books are filled with names we cannot pronounce and stories which hope to make American kids relate more to those in other countries than to their neighbors across the street.

I was completely surprised when, at the beginning of the second week of elementary school, the kids brought home their new textbooks emblazoned with the words "Common Core" on the front cover. My stomach immediately turned over as I began to read through the stories, feverishly searching for the bold Progressive agenda I had heard so much about.

The problem was, upon first reading, I couldn't find anything that outright made my blood boil. This is when I became extremely worried, as this is how the Left works. While we hate the Left when they slap us upside the head with their anti-American rhetoric, at least we can identify it. America's education system has become weakened because of the highly crafted Liberal logic hidden among traditional teachings in rewritten history books . . . as in the case of Hillcrest High School in Simpsonville, South Carolina, which includes a disputable definition of the Second Amendment. In the eleventh grade textbook, the Second and Third Amendments are combined and the summary just speaks about how we have a right to "bear" arms and omits the word "keep."

Liberals also are doing everything they can to incorporate a radical green agenda which includes watching and scolding parents when they are "environmentally unfriendly." In a recent article in the *New York Times*, a social worker in Dobbs Ferry, New York, said, "They're on my case about getting a hybrid car. They want me to replace all the light bulbs in the house with energy-saving bulbs."

Let's not forget the recent examples where the First Amendment rights of Christian or Conservative students were restricted as in the case of a group of high school athletes suspended for "Tebowing" in the hallway. Almost like a snake in the grass, slithering silently until he is right up next to you and ready to strike, this type of deceitful indoctrination is extremely dangerous as most parents today don't have time to read and analyze every little inch of their children's education. By the time we figure out where our child's mind has been wrongly persuaded, it's too late.

I applaud those outside the Common Core movement for exposing the wrongs of the program; however, I wonder if their energies would be better served if they were used to fight for private-school vouchers instead. I imagine once textbooks were printed and passed out to students, the idea of Common Core was pretty much tattooed onto today's education system. Our only hope is to be able to have as much control over what our children learn and, as of now, only private schools offer that ability. Unfortunately, the cost of private school tuition has increased to almost as much as a college. For most people, like our family, a private education is not a possibility.

The real lie about Common Core is that it is not about numbers or raising standards. If this was true, the admitted Progressive mayor of New York City, Bill De Blasio, would not have shut down the Success Academy chain of charter schools that included his most productive and highest grade averaging school. Common Core's main goal is about making our children more emotional and teaching them to lean on their feelings, not the facts. In many classes, students are allowed to take and retake a test until they feel good about the grade given.

THE REAL LIE about Common Core is that it is not about numbers or raising standards. Common Core's main goal is about making our children more emotional and teaching them to lean on their feelings, not the facts.

At a Greater Good Summer Institute for Educators event, one of the attendees was highlighted because she started out each day in her classroom asking the students how they were currently feeling. Students who replied they were feeling "out-of-sorts" were given time to visit the "balancing table" where they could draw or write in order to help them feel better. This is exactly what the Democrats want because they know feelings are much easier to manipulate and control.[7]

Progressives want children's opinions and decisions to be based not on facts and figures but on sympathy and passion. Emotions can be manipulated; facts and figures don't lie. The Democrats know their agenda and their message is false when you look at it in a black-and-white manner. Cuba, China, and Russia are prime examples of the Progressive (can we say Communist?) agenda. They know they have to find a way to appeal to the future voter based on devaluing truth while emphasizing emotion.

The Cost of Kids

As if we didn't have enough to worry about with the educational, health, social, and spiritual aspects of our children's lives, one of the biggest worries is whether people can *afford* to have children. The joke used to be that kids were a great tax deduction; however, the dollars per kid that I get back don't even come close to what it costs to clothe, feed, educate, and raise my offspring in this day and age. According to the latest estimates released by the US Department of Agriculture in 2013, the estimated cost for a middle-income couple to raise a child born last year until they are eighteen is $241,080. That is 3 percent higher than the 2011 estimate and doesn't even include the cost of college tuition.

What makes the budget even tighter for families today is that wages are not going up and household median incomes have fallen by more than $4,000 since 2000. Health care, education, and child care are elements that have increased the most. The combination of child care and education alone take up 18 percent of most household incomes. This is why income from today's families must come from more than just one parent. How can a family survive on just one salary when you always wish for your children to have better than what you grew up with?[8]

The idea of an inheritance is almost just as humorous as a company offering benefits like a 401(k) package and stock options.

Some folks say money is not as precious as time with children. But ask the parents of one of the homeless families—which account for 41 percent of the overall number of homeless people in America today—whether they would prefer to have time with their children or money to provide shelter, food, and health care for their family, and they would quickly answer "the dollars."

But have no fear, the "all-compassionate" government knows this problem in today's family and can't wait to swoop in and save the day, or at least make the American people think so. This administration, along with all of its minions, knows this is a great opportunity to gain and guarantee voters. By accomplishing all of their goals, using the umbrella of compassion (i.e., helping today's family survive under a struggling economy), the villain is hailed as a hero. Perfect Saul Alinsky tactics: create a crisis . . . solve the crisis . . . hail yourself the hero.

Ronald Reagan once said, "We don't have a trillion-dollar debt because we haven't taxed enough; we have a trillion-dollar debt because we spend too much."

Let's point out one big part of this quote.

Just a little over two decades after Reagan's statement, we have a *sixteen trillion* dollar debt, which is quickly approaching seventeen trillion. We have more than forty-eight million people on food stamps, with just over twenty-six million unemployed or underemployed people, and no realistic solution being proposed by those in office.

The Problem with Food Stamps

It is obvious that the food-stamp program is out of control. The federal government has expanded the program so much that American citizens as well as schools have become dependent on it. The food and milk industry wholeheartedly encourages the expansion because they stand to make hundreds of millions of dollars off of it, and employs an army of lobbyists on the Hill. Often, reelection campaign coffers are filled in return for the promise of growing WIC and other food-stamp programs.

There is no end in sight to this ever-expanding program. The American people must make entitlement reform a major issue in the 2014 and 2016 elections. Americans are very skeptical that real reforms could ever occur, as never in history has government enacted laws that reduce the power of a bureaucracy and increased that bureaucracy's efficiency.

A common-sense solution that most mothers would agree with would be to apply the same reasoning we use in our household budgets to the national budget. Time limits, work requirements, and limiting waste are obvious options. Why can people take advantage of the system and figure out how to fraudulently buy items like cigarettes and lottery tickets on food stamps? Until we make decisions based on what's good for the majority rather than the emotions of the minority, we will continue to see this problem grow.

Let's create a system that motivates independence. Let's reward those who go out and obtain work and pay into the system with incentives, whether it be with education, tax breaks, or other items which will help them climb the ladder of success.

Independence is not what this administration is striving to create. In fact, the Democrats have realized they can use entitlement programs and taxpayer dollars to thank their constituents and buy future voters.

Looking at the numbers, the states with the largest populations on food stamps are the same states with the highest voter turnout for Democrats and Obama in 2012. Many in the Liberal Left media like to brag that the majority of food stamp recipients reside in red states; however, their numbers are spun to reflect the percentage of a state's population. In reality, if you look at actual population numbers, New York, California, Michigan, and Illinois boast the largest amount of residents on food stamps—and I don't think it is a coincidence that these states also are considered to be solid Democrat states.

Approximately sixty-two million people voted for Obama, and on the day he was reelected there were around forty-seven million people on food stamps. I think it is safe to say the majority of these people will never vote for a Republican president—or any Republican candidate for that matter—as long as we are having the rightful discussion about how to reduce the number of people taking advantage of the system. The Democrats have done a fantastic job of "buying" voters through entitlement programs like welfare and food stamps and now we are looking at second and third generations of families in this system.

President Johnson started the food stamp program in 1964 under the "Great Society" plan and since then only under Presidents Reagan (due to a large employment boom) and Clinton (due to the 1995 Welfare Reform Act that was only signed by Clinton at the urging of his advisors to guarantee reelection) has the actual number of food stamp recipients been reduced.

Today, for every vote created by the Obama jobs plan, seventy-five went on food stamps and, more than likely, the Republicans will never be able to win back the majority of those bought-off votes. With generations of families on food stamps, the Democrats' goal of creating guaranteed future Democrats seems to be working.

The American dream is not about being born with a silver spoon in your mouth. Rather, the American dream is about finding a way to earn the silver spoon and use it . . . which should be one of the key lessons and motivations of every parent in the instructions they give their children.

THE AMERICAN DREAM is not about being born with a silver spoon in your mouth. Rather, the American dream is about finding a way to earn the silver spoon and use it.

Changing Roles

Parenting has always been about sacrifice. If you are motivated to provide, by your standards, the best environment in which your children will be raised, and it requires a double salary, then your work is just as noble outside the home as in. However, the lie that Democrats try to purvey is that Conservatives are against the mother being the dominant income provider. This might have been somewhat true in the past, but because of today's economic situation, couples are quick to take any opportunity, even if it means the more traditional roles are reversed.

"It takes a village" is one of my favorite quotes even though I despise the women who said it. In my world, while I have two children of my own, very rarely does a week go by that I am not in some way caring for my nieces or nephews who live just down the street. The same can be said about caring for my children.

Just as in my case, my sisters-in-law have very demanding jobs with unorthodox working hours and travel schedules. Over the last eight years, we have all filled in for each other when needed, whether it be for school pickups, homework help, or a sick child. A need instantly filled but never directly stated as our own working mother's guilt was lessened with the justification that the kids were not being shuffled around, but rather spending quality time with family.

The men of our family all pretty much work together in the family building business and have varied levels of domestic responsibilities. Never have I heard a protest that taking daughters to dance or changing diapers was "women's work"; these men do what is needed to ensure as healthy an environment as possible for the offspring. I consider it a blessing to have a support system so relatively close and I am amazed when I hear stories of dual working parents who are isolated from family and help and yet they still manage to make it work with very little protest outside of the home.

This is what is so peculiar to me about the Liberals who say that Republicans have a stereotypical mold that we fit our families in. Just the implication of a mold is insulting to Conservatives as today's family appreciates every role the mother and father serves and doesn't define or value one more than the other.

My mother was a career woman and for the first three years of my life, I was at home with my daddy. Often he tells stories of taking mirrors off the wall to let me crawl on, or pushing me down the greenway by Buford Highway on a pretty day in Atlanta. He was organic and made homemade baby food before the celebrity parents made it chic; mother still brags to this day about his teaching me to sing "Happy Birthday" for her before I turned one.

Later on Mother decided to quit work and stay home with me; however, I knew their budgets were greatly reduced as my father's painting and remodeling jobs could never compete with my mother's corporate world salary. I watched them struggle for years financially, and like most couples, this was usually the subject of their arguments.

Around my high school years, I started to resent my mother and these arguments, as I couldn't understand why she didn't go back to work if she was so valuable and could bring in the money to stop their financial woes. Day after day in the hot sun or the cold winters, I would see my father dress in his white-with-paint-splattered clothes and go out the door in the early morning carrying just his lunchbox, decorated with my paint pen artwork, and his thermos of coffee. It wasn't until I was older and I realized that, as hard as it was for Daddy to get up in the morning, there was no happier moment than when he came home to find my mother sitting at the kitchen table, peeling vegetables for the evening dinner, and laughing with me about my day.

"No" is Not Enough

While all generations have had their challenges in regard to how parents were able to teach their children, today's parent doesn't really get the option of just giving a straight no for an answer. I believe that thanks to technology, this generation might be the one that is smarter than its parents. These children have grown up with information at their fingertips and, as technology continues to advance, the smart parent has to keep up with the current advances. Pretty soon, there will probably be a good-parenting app you can download that automatically updates us on everything our kids are doing and thinking at all times. But until then we just have to keep checking our iTunes or Google Play receipts to see what our kids are purchasing.

It is because of these advances, that we have to stay not only current on what our children have, but more importantly on how they know to use it. I am not the first one to say that I am glad social media was not around during my college years. Growing up in the house of a trained lie detector, I will be the first to admit I learned how to make sure my tracks were covered if I was not where I should be. Even then, I would be overcome with guilt, knowing that if I was ever caught being dishonest, the wrath I would face would far outweigh any unauthorized fun I was able to get away with.

The same goes for kids today. While in the beginning social media was used to snoop or catch our kids doing wrong, enough time has gone by for kids to figure out how to save pictures and post later, giving the impression they are somewhere they are not. When I was a kid, all we needed to worry about was having a friend or, more importantly, a friend's parents vouch for us. In today's world, once a parent realizes they have been living under a false sense of security, it's hard to regain the feeling of trust because we know there are more tools to help lead our children astray than there are ways for us to keep them on the straight path.

This is why today's parent must be more willing to be open with explanations of actions and consequences. We can't just say no. Rather, we need to explain the results of their actions and do our best to encourage our children to make the right choices or face the consequences. We can't just use blanket threats and harsh words as kids today have been trained very well on quick comebacks and smart remarks, thanks to the majority of shows geared for this generation.

TODAY'S PARENT MUST be more willing to be open with explanations of actions and consequences. We can't just say no. Rather, we need to explain the results of their actions and do our best to encourage our children to make the right choices or face the consequences.

Have you watched any of the recent shows on Disney Jr., The Hub, or ABC Family? These shows are more scandalous than soap operas in some cases and the lack of respect for adult figures is scary . . . not to mention the style of dress of most of the girls looks like what Julia Roberts wore in the hooker scenes of *Pretty Woman*.

Still, we as parents are surprised when our children fire back sharp remarks and attitudes. Strong-willed children have always existed throughout time; however, never before have they had role models so easily available to misguide their attitudes and opinions.

Direction for the Future

Parents today are also parenting a generation of kids who are used to everyone on the team being given a trophy and the concept of bullying is being bullied itself. I don't like the idea of kids being hurt or names being called; however, that is called "life" and sometimes life just simply stinks. With every tear that is shed because of an injustice, character is built and strength to overcome is grown. My mother used to always tell me that "success is the best revenge" whenever I encountered a set of mean girls or had been made fun of. This was her way of channeling my negative emotion to good. The best thing we as parents could teach our children as a whole would be the concept that adversity breeds character.

Kids today haven't been allowed to build up that confidence because they have been praised for mediocrity; therefore, when a child does not receive praise or, even more dangerous, receives a criticism, the child doesn't know how to deal with the negativity properly. Eventually, the child harbors all of this negativity into a ball of emotion, which sometimes can lead to acting out in very dangerous ways. Many times, these children are given medication to control their emotions; however, without dealing with the cause of the emotion, the damage to the child's mind-set is not something that can be easily repaired.

In each of the cases where young people have been involved in mass killings on school grounds, the culprit had a history of mental disorders and in most cases was on a prescription treatment. This is a fear parents face every day as they send their children off to school, a fear that previous generations did not have to face.

Most parents have faith and trust that our children are safe when and where they are receiving their education. Now with Common Core, we have to worry about the dangers of what they are learning. With this new society of overly prescribed, sensitive children looking to seek revenge on their bullies and with disregard for any innocent victims, parents truly have to live by faith and prayer every morning when they send their children off to school, regardless of whether they live in small-town Iowa or urban Chicago.

With every generation, the snowball of society continues to roll and I have to wonder what parenting will look like when it is my children's turn. What values do we hold dear today that will be perverted, thus becoming the normal standard for the next generation of parents to deal with?

My biggest fear is that the government will continue to weave in and out of the family dynamic until we will no longer be able to make choices according to our own discernment. Future parents will only be there to serve as enforcers and moderators of a predetermined path for their children.

Sounds a little sci-fi doesn't it? But what else should we expect from a government that uses our own dollars to enslave us and capture our loyalty?

On the day my first child was born, like almost every other mother, I looked into my baby's eyes and made the solemn vow to protect, provide for, and love that child with every breath in my lungs and every bone in my body. All good parents today have at some point made that same vow. I can assure you that whether it is the Progressive Left infiltrating the school hallways or the elected Socialist trying to buy votes while weakening the family structure, they will quickly learn to never mess with a Conservative momma grizzly either outside or inside her cave. While all mothers make mistakes, truth is just as there is no definition of a perfect kid, there is no definition of a perfect mother.

I am a proud member of the mommy mafia; however, I cannot promise that I not will have a horse head in my bed the morning after this book is published for disclosing some of our secrets. The mob has its ways of handling anyone who gets out of line. Granted, it might be a picture from a *My Little Pony* book, but it will send the same message!

CHAPTER FIVE

Not Just a Girl and Her Gun

W<small>E ALL REMEMBER</small> the "War on Women," right? Yes, that cleverly crafted narrative that took hold in 2012 was certainly a stroke of genius. While America bickered about the Republican party's War on Women, the voters were too distracted to witness the *real* war on women.

It was a preposterous narrative; overnight, the media took hold of the talking points and never let go. Suddenly, it was an abuse of the finer sex that Conservatives did not want to pay for Sandra Fluke's birth control.

Overnight, those who raised very serious questions about abortion issues were part of this fictitious War on Women. People were labeled as misogynists overnight when they did nothing more than suggest that those with religious principles should not be forced to fund abortions.

But hey, Democrats couldn't very well run on the truth, could they? It was a far better tactic for President Obama to label his Mormon opponent as some backward misogynist than it would have been for him to admit some plain truths—that after four years, the economy had continued to sour, America's foreign policy was in shambles, and the "administration of transparency" was a flat-out lie.

All politicians lie, but the War on Women meme was particularly outlandish.

But it worked.

As women of all political persuasions bickered about the fictitious War on Women, they neglected to note the very serious war on women that has been taking place for decades.

The Real War on Women

While women debated the merits of taxpayer-funded contraceptives, many of us just turned our heads from the most obvious governmental assault on women: the routine disarmament of women.

For decades, the government has worked tirelessly to restrict our Second Amendment rights. Somehow believing that a disarmed society is immune from violence, the gun grabbers of the nation never seem to stop and think about what a firearm does.

When the gun grabbers stop and think about guns in the hands of citizens, they conjure images of gangbangers shooting it out on the streets of inner cities. They cringe to think of Right-wingers "clinging" to their guns. They imagine "gun nuts" and modern day militias in the hills of Idaho.

But they *always* neglect to mention a very important group: those who need an equalizer.

For the woman walking to her car down a dark alleyway or the mother of two who keeps a .38 snub in her dresser drawer, a firearm can serve (and has served) as a last line of defense between her and a criminal who does not care about law and order.

For the woman walking to her car down a dark alleyway or the mother of two who keeps a .38 snub in her dresser drawer, a firearm can serve (and has served) as a last line of defense between her and a criminal.

If we're going to talk about a War on Women, we should address the *real* war on women: the disarming of women.

What a Firearm Does

I'll be candid: I don't come to this discussion free of bias. Like many Southern girls, I have been around guns all my life. My daddy had them and his daddy had them. When I married a military man, I knew that with him came talks of "good prices" on ammo and repeated discussions between him and his friends about the pros and cons of AK's gas piston system versus the AR's system and the obnoxious, tangy smell of

Hoppe's No. 9 gun cleaner. And though that less-than-pleas-
ant aroma seems to linger long after the gun-cleaning kit has
been put away, I wouldn't have it any other way.

That's what Febreze is for.

I've been around guns all my life so I never developed the
fear of them that so many men and women have. I never pre-
sumed that one would simply "go off"; I always knew handling
them with respect was the answer to preventing accidents. Of
course, accidents do happen, but we've all seen a wreck on the
side of the road and yet we get in our cars each day.

The point? Guns are neither good nor bad; they're tools.
Be careful handling firearms, circular saws, kitchen knives,
and really *anything* that can hurt someone . . . but don't be
afraid to handle them.

The Gun Myth

If we allow the Liberals to dominate the discussion surround-
ing firearms, we can only see that firearms are instruments of
destruction. They are for criminals to engage in their illicit
dealings; they are for military members to kill the enemy. To
listen to Piers Morgan and the like, firearms are like tanks or
flamethrowers—they have no real application in civilian life.

Sure, you get the occasional Liberal who wishes to appear
reasonable and will frame the Second Amendment as a hunting consideration. We'll get to that later.

Firearms *can* be an instrument of destruction . . . in the
wrong hands. Criminals everywhere use them to wreak havoc

on populations. If we can accept that this is an imperfect world, we should be able to accept that danger looms and that good people have a right to self-preservation.

Firearms do not only help the nefarious; they help the law-abiding. They serve as an equalizer.

I carry a firearm. Not all the time, but I certainly retain the option. I have a permit to do so and I comply with the letter of the law.

In short, I'm one of the "good guys."

Last year, I sat down with a friend of mine I hadn't seen in a few months for dinner at a restaurant. We rarely agree on politics, so we tend to avoid such issues, but she couldn't help herself.

"I just don't know why people need guns. I get it for police or military use and I'm okay with hunters having them."

"Oh, that's kind of you to be 'okay' with hunters being allowed to have them," I interrupted.

Not noticing my sarcasm, she continued. "Yeah, but the simple fact is that having guns around just produces more violence. It's so sad that [Sandy Hook shooter Adam Lanza's mother] was killed, but if she didn't have these guns around, the kid would have never had access to them!"

I listened for a few more moments, trying not to be rude and letting her finish her point. Suddenly, I had reached my threshold for the amount of idiotic musings I could stand in the span of a few minutes and politely pushed back.

"That's really not true," I began. "Guns don't produce violence any more than kitchen knives produce meals. They're just tools."

"But if we didn't have them, people couldn't inflict massive damage," she insisted.

"Mass violence was invented with the firearm? So all those deaths by sword prior to guns were fairy tales? Do the Crusades ring a bell? What about the Boston marathon bombing? 'If nobody had pressure cookers, we wouldn't see this kind of violence.'"

My friend was not amused, and we both saw the futility of trying to convince the other. But before we moved to another subject, she tried to close out the discussion by asserting, "I just think it's sad. People feel they need guns because they're fearful of what's out there and those who carry guns are putting us all at risk."

"Putting us all at risk?" I inquired. Finally, I had had enough. "We've been talking for what, about an hour or so?"

She nodded.

I put my petite purse onto the table between us and calmly said, "We've been here for an hour and I've had a pistol in my purse this whole time."

Lisa's eyes went wide.

I continued, "In that time, how many people have I shot? How many times have I brandished my weapon? How many scenes did I cause?"

She said nothing.

"I carry a firearm because after we're done here, I'm walking to my car . . . alone. Down a couple blocks on a dimly-lit street. I'm scrappy, but I don't think I'm much of a match for a six-foot-two man, much less multiple men if they wanted to hurt me. My gun is an equalizer because, though they might be bigger than me, they're not more powerful than a .357. I carry a gun for the same reason I carry snow chains . . . I hope I don't have to use it, but if I do, I'll be glad I had it."

The discussion awkwardly transitioned to other things. I still value her friendship. What I hope, however, is that this bit of insight helped show her that the way she was thinking about firearms and, more importantly, how she was thinking about those who carry them was perhaps too simplistic for this complex world.

The Second Amendment Is Not Negotiable

"I'm okay with guns for hunting . . . "

"Why does someone *need* (insert any scary-sounding gun here)?"

"The Founding Fathers never intended for us to have assault rifles."

We've all had friends (and foes) say these kinds of things, right? Some distant cousin once heard some scary-sounding statistic and ended their antigun diatribe with one of the above assertions. How many of us have winced when we heard these things but out of decorum just let it go?

The Second Amendment is remarkably clear. It states:

> A well regulated Militia, being necessary to the security of a free State, the right of the people to keep and bear Arms, shall not be infringed.

Ah, it's refreshing to see that once upon a time, lawmakers kept things simple. Obamacare is tens of thousands of pages long; our right that protects all the others is twenty-seven words long. And Liberals call themselves "Progressives"!

IT'S REFRESHING TO see that once upon a time, lawmakers kept things simple. Obamacare is tens of thousands of pages long; our right that protects all the others is twenty-seven words long. And Liberals call themselves "Progressives"!

Feel free to reread the Second Amendment and underline in this book anyplace where it discusses hunting rights. Highlight anyplace that offers a description of what *kind* of guns are protected. Circle any part that gives any indication as to whether the Founding Fathers intended to only protect certain kinds of firearms.

No? No notations? That's because the Second Amendment is very clear. It is a tremendous provision that, while remarkable in its brevity, says so much.

The first part, detailing the need for militias, has long been the saving grace for gun grabbers. For decades, anti-gun crusaders pushed to advance the notion that the Second

Amendment protects the right to arm militias which, in contemporary speak, means the National Guard.

Not quite.

While a standing army has been important for America's defense, the need for a well-armed citizenry has been equally important. The militia of which the Second Amendment speaks is not the National Guard, but the assembly of patriots who are willing to gather to repel invasions. They were the patriots who stood at Lexington and Concord. They were the snipers and guerilla fighters who fought with Francis Marion—better known as the Swamp Fox—to repel the British throughout the South.

The militia is not an organized, standing military force; our militia is the armed citizenry. Throughout history, enemies have avoided invading our soil for a very simple reason: not only would they have to contend with the strongest military force known to man, but they would have to contend with millions of gun owners. Grandmas with handguns, ranchers with rifles, college students with Glocks—the threat of an intense guerilla war has just been too much for the enemies of America. We haven't been invaded since the War of 1812.

After decades of fighting to prop up the ludicrous notion that the Second Amendment supports a collective right to gun ownership, the 2008 Heller decision from the Supreme Court dashed the fading dreams of antigunners when they declared gun ownership to be an expressly individual right.

Liberals scrambled and came up with a new narrative. Instead of framing the issue as a protection of the militia, they reframed it as an issue of "individual ownership" . . . so long as the government gets a say.

"Commonsense gun control" became the new catch phrase for Liberals. As the Left began to drop its pretenses that the Second Amendment protected militias, it simultaneously adopted the even more absurd position that the Second Amendment protects individual firearm ownership, but allows for "commonsense" restrictions on such ownership.

And who decides what is and what is not "commonsense," you ask? Well, naturally, the government decides.

Please take out a marker and circle on the Second Amendment where it says anything about "common sense" restrictions.

It's a new twist on an old idea. When government doesn't want someone to use their right, they provide certain "reasonable" restrictions.

When the Jim Crow South didn't want blacks to vote, did they outlaw voting? Heck, no! They just put up restrictions to keep them from voting while saying, "Nobody's saying you can't vote; we just need 'commonsense' voting restrictions."

Likewise with this civil right, anti-Second Amendment advocates are employing the same old tactic.

Of course we all want to keep crazy people from hurting others, but government intervention is not the solution. If someone poses a danger to society, there are mechanisms to allow for institutionalization. However, if we accept that "crazy" people aren't allowed to have firearms and then we accept that government gets to decide who is and who is not crazy, then when we connect the dots, we see that the government decides who gets to own a firearm.

Sneaky, sneaky, Uncle Sam.

Furthermore, the Left is fighting this battle on a cultural level. With the help of the Liberal media, anti-gun-rights proponents have tried to shift the burden onto the American people to explain why they need their Second Amendment right.

"Why do you *need* an AR-15?" they'll ask. However, if you'll notice, they never seem to ask these same kinds of questions about other essential liberties.

For instance, they never seem to ask, "Why do you *need* to speak freely?" Our Second Amendment right is not subject to explanation any more than our First Amendment right.

Why do I need a firearm?

Because I do. Next question?

Another tricky way the Left tries to reframe the narrative in its own terms is by offering a viable reason why one would need a firearm, but limiting its usage.

"Why do you *need* an AR-15? They're not good for hunting, so they can only be good for killing humans."

Ugh . . . this is such an inherently deceptive position. The Second Amendment does not protect only those firearms that are useful for hunting. That's like saying that the First Amendment only protects conversations that are happy.

When Leftist loonies position their argument in this way, it's tough to take them seriously. If the Second Amendment was about hunting, then offering explanations for what kind of firearm they're using makes sense.

But what on God's green earth has possessed people to focus on hunting as the primary purpose when discussing Second Amendment issues?

Of course many, many people all around the globe use firearms to hunt. That's great. There's nothing wrong with that. In fact, a hundred years ago (or more), people did not have separate types of guns for hunting than they did for protection. Their guns were used universally as tools to solve many problems and needs. This is why the Second Amendment goes so much deeper than protecting the right to hunt; it protects the right to self-defense and national defense.

The brief amendment takes the time to show that this right is meant as a protection of the "security of a free state." It says nothing about protecting the means by which one can secure delicious dinners for their family. The sooner the Left moves off of this ridiculous notion that our firearm choices should be defended through the context of hunting, the better off we all will be.

Then, there are those who want to pretend that so-called "assault weapons" are outside the protection of our right to bear arms. People will verbally attack these scary-looking rifles and their owners and claim that the Founding Fathers never could have imagined that this amendment would have protected the right to such inventions as AR-15s and high-capacity magazines.

Our Founding Fathers likely never envisioned conversations taking place over cell phones, yet these conversations are protected by both the First and Fourth Amendments. Technology improves, society marches on, and if the Founding Fathers had only been referring to flintlock muskets, they would have said "flintlock muskets."

A Predictable Cycle

Tragically, America has gotten into a perverse rhythm. The details change, but the outline remains the same:

- A nut job shoots a bunch of people at a school, a mall, a movie theater, wherever, and the cycle begins.
- Newscasters scramble to find something, anything, to explain this situation and cling to whispered rumors and unsubstantiated facts.
- Often, biased "journalists" (and I use that term loosely) will vaguely speculate that perhaps the shooter was a Right-winger. They won't commit fully, but will plant the notion subtly. They will always speculate as to what firearms were used, even before anything is definitively known, and these hack journalists are always willing to "spice things up" by adding all kinds of scary adjectives. "Assault rifle," "assault weapon," "military-style rifle," "high-capacity

magazine," "military-style black rifle"—these grue-some propagandists will jump to the forefront of American coverage and sensationalize horrendous tragedies all to set the stage for a renewed gun-control push.

- Four, six, eight hours after the shots have been fired, it happens . . . someone boldly suggests that America needs to "have a conversation" about enacting fur-ther gun-control measures.

And as Americans grieve, Liberal vultures poise to push more government control as the answer to gun violence. They get a move on because the nation's shock and sorrow could wear off any minute and frightened moms, dads, brothers, and sisters could awaken to the fact that their rights are being slowly stripped from them under the guise of compassion.

It's truly revolting.

Nowhere has this pattern of behavior been more obvious than in the immediate aftermath of the shooting in Newtown, Connecticut, in late 2012.

Every parent in America felt the horrible cringe—that im-mediate feeling of intense anger mixed with an emotion that could only be described as heartbreak. Children—innocent, blossoming human beings—were gunned down and it was truly horrific. Parents across this country that night hugged their child for at least a second longer or read an extra bedtime story just because they were reminded of how blessed they were to have their children safe in their arms.

As awful as it was, most parents will understand when I say there was a brief, awful feeling of simultaneous sadness and gratefulness. In an instant, I felt shocked, then truly sad, then, for a moment, grateful that my son and daughter were safe and sound, and then guilty for the blessings I have while other moms and dads had been robbed. It happened all at the same time and it was a horrible feeling millions of parents felt all across the country.

But like everything else, the Progressives of this country used tragedy to promote their own ulterior agenda and should be ashamed for their exploitation of the victims and the pain felt by their families.

Celebrities, politicians, and media pundits—many of them have children. They were not immune to the heartache felt by "everyday" people. I too was angry and hurt by what happened and the natural response was to do something—anything—to keep this kind of tragedy from happening again. However, the hypocritical part of many of these people is that they hire or are provided protection in the form of bodyguards or security teams who typically carry a firearm.

But the immediate aftermath of a national tragedy was not the time to dust off the old gun-grabbing agenda. When a family member dies, someone, at some point, should decide what to do with their estate; however, greedily vying for the painting down the hall before the body is even cold is just plain disrespectful.

Similarly, while I hugged my children tighter the next few days, our television was bombarded with reactionary Liberals using this moment as the time to push their antigun agenda.

Days and weeks went by with more of the same. Actors demanded action on the issue of gun violence which, naturally, meant increased governmental control; MSNBC and CNN blasted any who dared to frame this as a constitutional issue, accusing them of being uncaring. Hysteria had taken the place of reasoned discourse.

The Gun Issue Hits Home

I owe almost all of my professional life to the gun debate which erupted in December 2013.

I had been in broadcasting for my entire adult life, but mainly in supportive roles. I had just recently been pulled in front of the camera by an online news show's producer in Atlanta, after filling in for a guest who did not show up. I had been blessed to have a few big-name interviews and even had a video go viral, but I had not been able to break onto the network news scene . . . not until Sandy Hook.

For the first time, my mother told me the truth about what had happened to Cliff. Her justification was that she could see our Second Amendment rights being under attack and the Left could not fight my words as they were coming from the voice of a victim of gun violence.

I wrote my column for Townhall titled "Smoke Pot, Ban Guns, Kill Kids." Soon I received a phone call from my publicist who, up until that point, I swear had promised to name his soon-to-be-delivered child after whichever TV host decided to give me my first break.

I will remember that phone call for the rest of my life because I don't think any other call has ever had a life-changing effect like this one. "I have good news and I have bad news," said Keith almost immediately.

"Okay," I said, bracing myself for another letdown.

He replied, "The good news is you are going to be on Piers Morgan's show on Monday night. The bad news is, you will be in front of a live, handpicked studio audience of around a hundred people, the only female, and probably the only one who will be defending the Second Amendment. Think you can handle it?"

The next four days were spent in what I consider to be prep-boot-camp hell. I memorized every fact possible, went through drilling by some top debaters, and practiced one-liners and on-my-feet comebacks, unsure what I might face on the set of Morgan's show.

He had been ruthless with other guests; I had seen my friends Ben Shapiro, Alex Jones, and Larry Pratt all be subjected to his mockery during their interviews for his "Guns in America" series. The best advice I was given came from my publicist, who said, "As long as you come out of the interview without crying or cursing, you have won."

I was blessed to have my former boss and close friend, talk-radio host Rusty Humphries, also in New York City during that time as he was doing a few media appearances on Fox News that same week. Rusty had been the one who really encouraged me to make the leap from behind the scenes, but while he didn't express it at any point, I knew even he was worried about sending me into the lion's den.

Finally, the night of the *Piers Morgan Live* show was upon me. While the staffers and, to an extent, Mr. Morgan treated me with respect, Morgan had developed a reputation for his brash, confrontational political punditry.

On January 15, 2013, a little over a month after the shooting at Sandy Hook Elementary, I joined a panel of respected pundits with various views on the Second Amendment. Nervous, I reminded Morgan that the Second Amendment is not only for use against home intruders and deer, but as a baseline threat to tyranny.

Like I had told my friend Lisa, I noted, "Evil is going to happen. They will find a way. If someone wants to do somebody harm, they're going to do it regardless of if they use a gun, a knife, or any sort of tool. And all [gun control] is doing is punishing the legal, good citizens of the United States and taking away rights that were given to us by our Founding Fathers."

Morgan questioned if the Founding Fathers could have conceived of an AR-15 rifle. I replied that these same visionaries likely did not conceive of the Internet or cable networks, but that we could not apply restrictions to one right without applying them to others.

The conversation moved on but we soon circled back to the Liberals' favorite argument; demanding that I answer his question, Morgan repeatedly asked, "Why do you need [an AR-15]?"

As I stated before, such questions are faulty at their core; they presuppose that the Bill of Rights is a Bill of Needs. However, our rights are divined from God, guaranteed by government, and enjoyed by citizens.

"Our Bill of Rights isn't a bill of needs; it says 'Bill of Rights,'" I retorted. Morgan pushed on, asking me to identify why I *needed* an AR-15, and I pointed out that the Second Amendment is a handy little tool for keeping despotic governments at bay.

"Let's look through history. Right now we might like our government," I began. "But you've got Cambodia, you've got Russia, you've got Germany . . . governments go corrupt!"

Almost not believing what he was hearing, Morgan responded, "Just to clarify, you believe an American government in the modern age is going to turn tyrannical?"

"I have the right to be able to own a gun just in case," I replied. "We don't know what's going to happen. Today, we might have a bright, sunny America. But who's to say what's going to happen."

At that moment, I could hear the faint sounds of Liberal heads exploding all around the country.

The notion was preposterous to those who could never conceive of a tyrannical American regime. The same people who called George W. Bush a dictator and warned of the "too-powerful executive branch" now seemed to fully trust the good intentions of the Obama regime that spoke freely about ordering "executive actions" on gun control to circumvent Congress. It was baffling.

Liberals pounced, reacting as if I were some camo-fatigue-attired militia member talking about the New World Order.

What I had said was simple and true: governments go corrupt sometimes. It may not happen tomorrow, it may not happen ever. But to implicitly trust that we would *never* need to take up arms against government agents in America is to deny the realities of government and to betray a naiveté about world history.

To IMPLICITLY TRUST that we would never need to take up arms against government agents in America is to deny the realities of government and to betray a naiveté about world history.

That night I had to face the parents of two of the children massacred at Sandy Hook, as well as a brother of one of those killed in the Aurora, Colorado, theater shooting. My heart ached for their grieving loss, but I knew that I could not let the emotion of the situation distract me from getting the message across. All this president was doing was weakening the ability for honest, law-abiding Americans to protect themselves.

Literally, within minutes of leaving the studio, I felt as if I had been hit by a Mack truck as the adrenaline which had kept me going for the previous four days left me. In its wake, the full-blown NYC flu was ready to take over what was left of my exhausted body. I knew that I had to make it through one more interview that evening on my friend David Webb's SiriusXM Patriot show and then I could succumb to the misery that was starting to overcome me.

Or so I thought.

As my luck would have it, the next day while I was preparing to board my Delta flight home to Nashville, half delirious with a 104-degree fever, my publicist received a call from Piers Morgan's producers asking if I would come back on the show that evening to continue the discussion. This time it would just be me in the studio with Morgan and radio talk-show host and CNN contributor Dana Loesch via satellite. My publicist knew how sick I was as I was forced to turn down other invitations all day due to my weakened state, but he told me that whatever it took, I had to make sure I did not miss this opportunity.

I had come to accomplish a mission; my job was not done yet. Hours later, I found myself back on set. This time it was just me face-to-face with Morgan, and he seemed less accommodating of dissenting opinions than he did the prior evening.

Together, Dana and I asserted some truths that seemed incomprehensible to the brash Brit who could not understand America's guaranteed right of individual gun ownership.

Morgan led off with the traditional "common-sense gun-control" issue of background checks. He asked why legal gun owners were rejecting the call for universal background checks that would interject government authority in everything from private sales to gifts of a hunting rifle between father and son.

I pointed out that I was a legal gun owner and had no problem passing background checks, but criminals who look to purchase firearms for illegal purposes do not go through the legal process to buy them. Thus, background checks are only useful for a government that wishes to keep track of the law-abiding citizens who own firearms.

Constantly trying to put the burden of proof on the American citizens, Morgan wanted to know where in the Constitution it said that we could own AR-15s, capable of firing many rounds quickly. Not falling into that line of thinking, I could only reply, "More importantly, Piers, where does it say that I cannot?"

The conversation quickly devolved into a discussion focused on the absurd. Repeatedly, Morgan asked me if I thought we should be able to own a tank. Over and over again, I was asked if we, as civilians, could own a tank.

Aside from the fact that civilians can, and do, own tanks, the size of the weaponry is not at the heart of the issue. Continually attempting to frame the *tool* as the true instrument of violence,

Morgan flailed as he focused on everything from AR-15s to tanks, never addressing the simple and oft-repeated truism: guns don't kill people; people kill people.

It was a hunting rifle that killed my brother. Is he less dead from having been shot with a "normal"-looking gun? Of course not. A knife, a handgun, an AR-15 . . . it doesn't matter; people get killed by other people looking to kill. Limiting the availability of effective weapons only affects those who wish to remain within the confines of the law.

Throughout all his blustering about tanks, Morgan missed the central point: murder is illegal. Nobody ever said, "Well, I was going to shoot up this school, but since there's laws against me possessing a firearm, I guess I won't." Whether it comes in the form of a tank or a Glock, we cannot escape evil by trying to limit access to weapons.

In fact, time and time again, the stats tell a different story.

A Wake-Up Call

While President Obama and his mindless toadies parrot the same old talking points about the need for increased gun-control measures, they miss the obvious facts. Many of these shootings occur in "gun-free zones" which, as the name suggests, are areas where guns are prohibited.

What criminal is okay with murder, but has a qualm about violating the sanctity of the "gun-free zone"? It makes no sense.

One of the defining moments in the struggle for the restoration of our Second Amendment rights came from a tragedy.

On October 16, 1991, George Hennard crashed his pickup into a Luby's Cafeteria in Killeen, Texas. The deranged man emerged from his truck and began executing patrons. Passing over many men in order to shoot women, the gunman, apparently driven by a hatred for women, shot fifty people, killing twenty-three.

As seventy-one-year-old Al Gratia rushed the madman, Gratia was shot in the chest. His wife, Ursula, cradled her dying husband and she too was murdered. Their daughter, Suzanna Hupp, escaped the massacre.

However, Hupp was allowed to legally carry her pistol. The Second Amendment supporter carried her pistol wherever she went, but had left her gun in the car to comply with the Texas law that prohibited carrying of concealed weapons in "public places."

What good is a gun if it cannot be carried in "public places"? Apparently not much good at all. Hupp reached for her gun but soon remembered that it was in the parking lot. Because Hupp complied with the law, many more were injured, many more were murdered, and Hupp had to witness the slaughter of her parents.

Hupp crusaded for the law to be changed, and in 1995, Texas changed its laws to reflect a more pro-Second Amendment stance. Now citizens may carry their concealed weapons in public places.

Still, many states that offer "shall issue" permits demand payment in order to issue the permits. They run background checks and demand that applicants take classes before being *allowed* to exercise their Second Amendment rights. While it is certainly a good idea to become acquainted with one's firearm, these requirements show that we have a long way to go before we can witness the realization of true liberty with regards to the Second Amendment.

The Bottom Line

The Second Amendment is not about a fascination with guns; it's not about hunting; it's not about "commonsense" restrictions. The Second Amendment serves as an underlying freedom that ensures liberty for all Americans.

Furthermore, it's important to realize that the fight over the Second Amendment represents the *true* war on women. As Liberals bicker with Conservatives about birth control, they refuse to empower women with the ability to defend themselves against attackers.

They talk about violence against women as if catchy bumper stickers alone will help stop rape or other assaults. They crusade for telecoms on university campuses for endangered women to alert security of threats, but simultaneously work to keep responsible students from carrying concealed weapons on campuses.

The true war on women is not about birth control or male-oriented pronouns; the true war on women is the systematic disarmament of women all across the country.

If we are going to get serious in this country about addressing the issues affecting women, we must start by fervently supporting the right of women (and men) to defend themselves.

We must not forget the numerous stories of how legal gun owners have saved their lives, their families' lives and, in many cases, the lives of strangers from a person wanting to do harm.

We must not forget the story of the mother who hid in the closet in her middle-class Atlanta, Georgia, home with her two children until the intruder found her and her children, and upon opening that closet door, found himself staring down the barrel of a .38 revolver. Knowing she and the children were in eminent danger, the mother promptly unloaded all six bullets in the chamber, striking the assailant in the face and neck area.

While we can never predict what might have happened, in this case, it is pretty safe to say the actions of this mother thankfully saved her family from possibly being an addition to the Gwinnett County morgue.

We must support concealed-carry reciprocity across the fifty states—legislation that requires all fifty states to recognize the concealed-carry permits issued in other states.

We must support concealed-carry on campuses all across the country. While many states have done this, this is one place where the federal laws could be useful as interstate travel can become tricky in non-carry states.

And most importantly, we must educate ourselves on this important issue and refuse to accept emotional rhetoric as a substitute for legitimate discussion. We must reject the preferred Liberal narratives and reject that we must explain why we *need* our Second Amendment right.

Why do I need a gun? Try and take it and you'll find out.

(PS: I am still looking for a tank!)

CHAPTER SIX

"The Fair and Balanced Media" . . . Said No One Ever

S HARYL ATTKISSON LEFT CBS News earlier this year because she was tired of the Liberal bias within their newsroom. This came on the heels of Russia Today TV anchor Liz Wahl quitting while on the air, where she cited that she could no longer "be part of a network funded by the Russian government that whitewashes the actions of Putin." More and more, the role of many in modern-day media is more substantial than ever as they try to establish a new hierarchy and rules of ethics in regard to handling the distribution of information.

I will be the first to admit that while I am usually one of those known for blurring lines when it comes to most subjects, I am a complete purist when it comes to broadcasting the news. I always wanted to be in broadcasting. My mother said she directed my attention to that profession because she realized when I was very young that I had a flair for the dramatic. My childhood friends were often the stars of my various plays or models in my runway fashion shows.

One of my favorite days ever was when my parents decided to buy a VHS camcorder. Remember the ones that weighed around ten pounds and the only editing you could do was rewinding and taping over what you just recorded? My parents had been saving for months to purchase this luxury item, but I quickly commandeered it from them to launch of my own talk show called *What's Up?*

The set of my talk show consisted of two swivel barstools that I kept in the basement when not in use, and my guest consisted of any girlfriend who dared have a slumber party at my house. I don't remember much from my in-depth interviews with these girls. I do remember once when I made my friend Alisha angry because I made her admit her crush and then asked what he might have done if he saw the tape. Alisha never came back on my show and she told all of our other friends not to go on my show because I was going to ask embarrassing questions.

I learned a very valuable lesson from that experience: Telling someone else's story is a privilege and extremely powerful. The problem is, power is easily corrupted and the power of the pen should only be used to advance the good and destroy the bad. In many cases, especially in small towns across America, the local newspaper is the only medium through which people can keep politicians from going corrupt. Sure, we look to these papers to let us know who won the chili cook-off at the local senior center or what local high-school football player is being signed to play at the local community college. But the true mission of local news outlets is to keep the politicians kosher.

Telling someone else's story is a privilege and extremely powerful. The problem is, power is easily corrupted and the power of the pen should only be used to advance the good and destroy the bad.

We always say the voting box is where people judge a candidate's merits, but where do you think the majority of information voters receive comes from? Your local media, and if there is no reporter focused on city hall or your local school board, I can guarantee corruption is running rampant.

Now, equally as dangerous as receiving no information about local elected officials and their actions, if not more so, is having the media in the pocket of the politicians and community leaders. This is exactly what has been happening at all levels of government in the past and why today's environment is ripe for a new sector of journalism to form.

Fact Versus Opinion

I went to school and studied journalism. I did internships. I volunteered for events and I took every opportunity possible to study those in the business. Even if it meant fetching coffee or sweeping floors, as long as I was able to be around the newsroom, I did it. I have worked hard for the opportunity to cover the events happening in the world today and I consider my professional purpose in life is to be a conduit for information to the people.

With the birth of the "citizen journalist," or "new media journalist," I believe it is up to those of us in traditional media or with an education in the communication business to set the example for this new category of press. We need to be sure that we identify our stories as either being purely fact or interjected with opinion. Most networks and print today have failed in keeping the two separate. There are ample chances for the press to have the opportunity to successfully have a balance of both fact and opinion, with clearly defined borders. Yet, it is rare that you find a news outlet which does so.

Media bias is guaranteed to exist and I honestly have no problem with it. The problem is, those on both sides of the aisle often refuse to admit they are prejudiced and, more importantly, what they say is oozing with bias. Most of the time when I give a speech, I try my best to make it a point in the beginning to admit that I am a biased journalist and while I believe my opinion is correct, it is still my opinion supported by these facts. Most in today's media refuse to acknowledge this, thinking it would hurt their credibility. I see it as the only way to restore credibility to the media. Let's face it: the only profession which the American people have less or equal trust in than Congress is the media. The sad part is, we in the business have done it to ourselves.

In many cases, today's viewer would like to have the opportunity to watch a newscast and receive just the facts—the who, what, where, and when of the story. However, just like everything else in today's culture, most stories while delivering these facts interject the "why."

I think the key element missing in today's media is respect—respect for the story being told, the people involved and most importantly the result or outcome of the story. We already know the online media outlets promote views and hits regardless of whether they are favorable or not. Unfortunately, it seems this is starting to creep into traditional media outlets as well. With the popularity of reality shows and the demand for excitement, newscasts are now finding ways to attract attention even if it means pulling off media stunts which used to only occur on shock-jock radio.

I THINK THE key element missing in today's media is respect—respect for the story being told, the people involved and most importantly the result or outcome of the story.

When Erick "Mancow" Muller decided in 1993 to shut down the San Francisco Oak Bay Bridge during rush hour so that his sidekick could receive a haircut, Conservatives applauded the publicity stunt. Mancow staged the publicity

stunt in response to President Bill Clinton practically shutting down the Los Angeles International Airport to get a
haircut from celebrity stylist Christophe on Air Force One.
While the stunt resulted in fines and community service for
the radio host, Mancow's name became a household name
and he later became a weekly guest on Fox's morning show,
Fox and Friends. However, after calling the former chairman
of the Democratic National Committee Howard Dean "vile,"
"bloodthirsty," and "evil," as well as claiming he was purposely
waterboarded live on air, Mancow's antics were considered
too shocking for the Conservative news station and his segment was cancelled.

Grabbing Today's Audience

Years later, while publicity stunts are not at full shock-jock
status yet, the same effect of gaining viral attention is done
with a more powerful weapon of journalists: words. Entire
shows are now built around trying to see who can make the
most outlandish comments or who can find a subject that will
cause a new phrase to be coined or cause a buzzword impossible for the other networks not to cover.

Fox's *The Five* is a great example of a show that, despite
being relatively new on the scene, boasts ratings that are competitive with many of its more seasoned counterparts, and
that are almost always higher than any of the other shows
on the competing networks. While many would say it's because the hosts are "telling it like it is," or not "sugarcoating"

how the American people feel, I attribute *The Five*'s success to the daggers they successfully carve and impale into all of the different arteries of the Liberal argument. However, unlike other shows that do it by snarling and growling, they repeatedly inflict their wounds wrapped either in Greg Gutfeld's well-crafted monologues or with smiles as sweet as molasses. Even their banter with the token Liberal Bob Beckel or Juan Williams is clothed in love as you can tell the other political hosts genuinely care for their Liberal friend on the panel.

CNN's *Crossfire*, on the other hand, would love to boast high ratings, especially considering its past success; however, the overall mistrust of many Republicans for CNN has been a real obstacle to overcome. Very few can debate the idea that the four panelists cover all of the spectrums of both political viewpoints. Having spent time with the Newt Gingrich campaign as well as currently working with many of his former staffers in my role at the Tea Party News Network, I honestly doubt there is a better example of a Conservative in media than the former Speaker of the House of Representatives. The more moderate S. E. Cupp does a good job of representing the intellectual younger Republican crowd; however, Cupp and Gingrich's Republican strengths are equally matched on the opposite end of the spectrum in their Liberal cohosts Van Jones and Stephanie Cutter.

This is why I think *Crossfire* might never have a chance of seeing the high ratings it formerly received. Plus, in the case of *Crossfire*, when political debate occurs, most Conservatives want to see the debate won overwhelmingly and consistently by the Republicans. This rarely happens on *Crossfire* as most discussions end in a draw, with the hope that the viewer will make the determination, appreciative of both sides' viewpoints being equally told. Ratings tell a different story at this point as *Crossfire* has yet to climb out of its current ratings hole.

Many might say the reason that Fox receives higher ratings is because more Republicans watch cable news than Democrats. But the truth is, Fox News continues to boast higher ratings on its network because Republicans today don't have as many options to receive their news as those on the Left. Without stating the obvious competition of MSNBC, other networks like Comedy Central are much more deceiving in their political influence.

Glenn Beck's TheBlaze TV is probably one of the closest competitors to the Fox News network and has done an incredible job of building a full schedule of shows with great hosts who boast viewpoints from Conservative to Libertarian. The momentum given TheBlaze TV is in large part due to the strong, opinionated message given by hosts such as Andrew Wilkow (early on) and Dana Loesch without fear of backlash from management. Beck also was one of the first in the media movement to create a true network of TV, radio, and online media and utilize the promotional benefits of all three. As TheBlaze TV continues to recruit other well-known Conservatives who might have been tempered at previous stations, I guarantee their success will continue to rapidly grow as it's obvious that Americans are thirsty for this type of programming.

You are going to continue to see other Conservative broadcasting outlets like One American News Network out of San Diego and Newsmax TV try to gain similar popularity and with the ability to attain a placement on satellite, it's certain that others will develop. This is especially important as this could be the new home for many terrestrial Conservative radio hosts in the future.

On November 15, 1989, Time Warner launched the Comedy Channel. The standard format for the Comedy Channel's shows involved various hosts introducing clips culled from the acts of stand-up comedians, as well as classic comedies of the 1970s and 1980s, such as *Young Frankenstein* and *Kentucky Fried Movie*, presented in a style similar to music videos. Then in 1997, the channel realized the potential for influencing politics through pop culture and comedy with the success of South Park and the limits continued to be pushed. Language, nudity, and pranks continued to get more obviously bold; however, all of those paled in influence when it came what really mattered: politics. Shows like *The Daily Show* with Jon Stewart and *The Colbert Report* started competing in viewer numbers with traditional news talk shows and the coveted guest spot became a priority for most candidates, knowing the large viewing audience an appearance would achieve.

If you don't think the Comedy Channel realizes its political power and doesn't purposely use it to sway voters and public opinion, then please explain their reasoning behind "partnering" with TRU Insights and Insight Research to conduct an extensive study seeking to "define, frame, and understand" what role humor plays in swaying the millennial voter's opinion. What is really interesting is that following the study, Comedy Central issued a press release which basically told the public that not only did Comedy Central realize its power, but they also liked to brag about it.

The following "key findings" are excerpted from their official press release:

- Do not underestimate Millennials; they are very aware of what's going on in politics. And they are involved and influential.
- When it comes to political comedies, they don't watch to get informed; they watch because they are informed.
- What a candidate thinks is funny tells Millennials who they really are.
- Politicians must leverage humor to connect with Millennials; this generation needs humor, and they're saying it will shape their votes. [9]

These bullet points alone I find humorous. The first is truly brown-nosing to the millennial generation; however, seeing that it is Comedy Central, I would have given them more credit if they had said:

- Do underestimate Millennials: they are very *un*aware of what's going on in politics. And they are *not* involved and influential.

The next bullet point continues the pandering; however, when you combine it with the following two points, you realize the public relations department basically insults millennials by saying they base their vote on whoever can tell the best version of "why did the chicken cross the road" . . . that a politician who can tell a good joke or performs a funny parody had the best chance of winning the majority of the fifty million votes of the millennial generation. Talk about a backhanded slap in the face to the millennial generation! Yet Comedy Central is brazen enough to issue a press release praising this point and no one calls them out for their insulting comments.

Where the real hypocrisy lies among the viewers of many of Comedy Central's shows—current and past—is that the same viewers who watch shows like *South Park*, *The Sarah Silverman Program*, *Halfway Home*, and any of the *Roast* specials are the first to scream "bigotry" and "blasphemy" at not only Conservative programming but at their hosts and frequent guests. In fact, Jon Stewart's show has recently seemed like simply a rerun of most Fox News shows, with the addition of his sarcastic comments. I even venture to say, deep in the hollows of Comedy Central there is a bat cave filled with Fox News and other Conservative outlet stalkers, just waiting to capture a line or a mistake they can bury away until needed for a segment months later. Obviously, some manager at Comedy Central sees this as a productive use of funds and it does produce great ratings; however, I just see it as being pathetic.

Respect, the Key Ingredient

Press outlets, which seem to consistently try to be respectful, are often rewarded with higher ratings. Recently, CNN decided to cancel Piers Morgan's prime-time show because of its failing numbers. Morgan's show didn't get low marks because it was a bad show or he was a particularly bad host. No one can dispute that Morgan had some of the best guests possible and his subjects were usually pretty on-target for what was happening that day. He received low ratings because he didn't have respect for his guests who differed from his opinion. He dismissed those who didn't share his train of thought and insulted people whose views were opposite of his. Hence, no one wanted to watch this public flogging of people who had a different outlook.

The top-rated political show, *The O'Reilly Factor*, has just as intense a host as Piers Morgan. Bill O'Reilly takes on those with opposite opinions with the same amount of tenacity but with a regard which doesn't make the audience feel pity for the guest and guilty for watching the host assault his visitors.

The same can also be said about the majority of hosts on the News Corp stations, which makes one think that while the hosts and contributors on those stations are diverse in their broadcast technique, respect is a shared attribute in all. This is evidently a qualification reiterated by management and probably looked for specifically by Roger Ailes when he chooses his talent, knowing that a network built on respect for differing opinions is guaranteed to succeed.

The same could be said about other network hosts like CNN's Anderson Cooper, HLN's Nancy Grace, and the majority of the lineup on CNBC. Respect for guests even when you differ in opinion produces good ratings and establishes the most important quality that a journalist aims to gain: *credibility.*

RESPECT FOR GUESTS even when you differ in opinion produces good ratings and establishes the most important quality that a journalist aims to gain: credibility.

With technology creating new ways of getting information out by the minute, the power and strength of online news sites continues to grow. Many of these websites boast reach and viewer numbers which compete and in some cases beat traditional broadcast mediums. Many consider this relatively new form of media to be their primary source for information, and because you can access this media at the time you wish and in the form you wish, many say this new form of media will continue to grow in dominance over the other forms. In fact, the timing of the rise of online media outlets and the fall of the print newspaper/magazine industry is too obvious to consider it just coincidental.

Websites like Drudge Report, The Daily Caller, Townhall, Breitbart and of course my own Tea Party News Network have tried to set up traditional management levels which not only make the writers accountable for the words they write, but also secure in the information they post. While the traditional newsroom might not exist in these news outlets because staff members are scattered around the country, the goals of these online news organizations and their reporters are the same. Instead of ratings, these outlets are judged by hits or social media shares. Having a news video or story go viral is always a prize sought by these news outlets, and the idea of cross-promotion with other websites seems to be more abundant than with the traditional media.

Credibility: Who Do You Believe?

The real problem with online websites that doesn't apply to larger organizations where there are levels of management is accountability. The real challenge lies in websites solely controlled by a single person or a very small group. Many times the number of people actually involved in these websites is small; however, that is not made obvious. Those same people may post anything they want about anyone they wish and it is truly up to the reader or followers of that website to decide how much credibility they give that information. Just as we don't believe that Al Gore created the Internet, it's easy for people to say, "Don't believe everything you read on the Internet," and yet folks do. The ironic part for Al is that I imagine at times, he wishes he had.

Please don't think I believe that every website just run by one or two people is corrupt, as I know several great examples which are more responsible in their fact checking than the larger operations. These websites are operated by good people who are doing it for the good of the cause and don't have any intentions of using their website to grow enormous bank accounts or to target others. Rather, they believe in getting as much of the truth and information to the people as possible. In some respects, these writers and these websites have taken on the role of the modern-day investigative reporter.

Nevertheless, I am afraid that the entire industry could potentially be discredited because not all people understand the power of the pen (or in this case, the keyboard). One major problem, which occurs often with everyone having the ability to reach the masses, is an environment where middle school behavior like gossiping, false accusations, and even bullying can occur. All it takes is one person posting on a forum, social media, or blog a comment about someone and others might take it as a truth.

This is extremely dangerous when we as Americans are already confused as to what is the truth. We live in a society where only a superficial level of respect is being taught and where hate is being encouraged as long as it's toward those defined by the Progressive as "haters." This past Super Bowl, Coca-Cola aired a commercial titled, "It's Beautiful." The commercial showed people of eight different ethnicities singing "America the Beautiful" as well as two dads roller-skating with their daughter. The ad was considered to be a disgrace and unpatriotic by many in the Conservative community and the criticism spread like wildfire on social media. Many on the Left countered the protest saying those criticizing were racist, homophobic, and anti-peace.

The ironic part is, just months earlier in New York City, I was floored to see an ad for now Mayor Bill de Blasio against Joe Lhota which basically demonized the Tea Party and its position on gun permits and delaying Obamacare, and saying they wanted to throw people on the streets of NYC. Yet, where was the outcry at this very inflammatory campaign commercial meant to encourage hate against anyone who claimed to be a member of the Tea Party? All we heard was silence and on Election Day, Bill became mayor.

The only ones who even began to cry foul and probably one of the only media where the majority can claim a Conservative majority is in talk radio. For years it has been discussed how talk radio all the way from the top with Rush Limbaugh down to the local radio host has been under assault from the Left. For years, it has been no secret that talk-radio hosts as well as Fox News and others have been the constant thorn in mainly the Democrats' side. However, sometimes

Republicans are the target of the usually friendly media. This unbiased reporting on the corruption of both sides makes many in office wish these truth-tellers would just disappear; however, with the failure of the Fairness Doctrine, politicians decided to find other ways to eliminate their biggest critics in the media—by eliminating their sponsors.

Did you ever wonder why, if Fox News is consistently the top-rated news cable network and often the top-rated cable network, the majority of its advertisers are selling either precious metals, catheters, or "as seen on TV" products? Yet, when I turn the channel to CNN, I find myself watching mainstream companies like Cadillac promoting its products? Why wouldn't a business want to promote its product where the top ratings are? Granted, this allows for local businesses to take advantage of forsaken inventory, and in most markets, Fox News as well as local radio stations have some of the highest cost-per-spots packages. However, the question still makes one ponder: how much influence does the government have on large business if it can make the marketing dollars move in the direction of its friends and stay away from its foes?

Our Responsibility

The good news is that no matter what influence Big Brother is trying to grow in the traditional media markets as well as using regulations to obstruct the non-traditional, there is one type of journalist who is a little bit more tricky to try and control: the citizen journalist.

Thanks to technology today, anyone can be a citizen journalist. With social media having no limitations in reach, today's average Joe citizen can influence just as many as those with a national microphone. Even more interesting is that today's citizen journalist actually has a stronger grip on making someone see from their viewpoint and accept their opinion than some stranger's. People today are lacking trust in the media; however, they still trust their friends and in this day and age, a friend's recommendation or comments are sometimes priceless in regards to an issue.

I love that everybody now has the opportunity to tell a story or to get information out via individual blogs or social media. Today more than ever before, there is more power for the individual to make a difference politically. In a world where cell phones can record studio quality video of either an action in public or a person's opinion, we have seen numerous videos go viral and catapult an unknown to becoming a household name.

EVERYBODY NOW HAS the opportunity to tell a story or to get information out via individual blogs or social media. Today more than ever before, there is more power for the individual to make a difference politically.

However, with this new ability to sway opinion comes great responsibility. If you have an iPhone or computer, you now have the opportunity to reach as many folks as those of us who have studied this craft for years. The possibility of being recorded at all times is now in the back of every public figure's and elected official's mind. While I believe we do still get slipups every once in a while, many politicians have become more closed and guarded than in years past, in fear of a mistake that could cause a public-relations nightmare.

Remember toward the end of the 2012 campaign, when then-Republican presidential nominee Mitt Romney was caught on a camera phone at a private fund-raiser saying that, "There are 47 percent of people who will vote for the president, no matter what"? Many on both sides of the aisle say this now infamous comment was the final and largest nail in his campaign coffin. A planned comment, recorded by phone camera; however, its instant viral circulation was not. Other comments made without thinking have been just as dangerous, but I believe we have become too sensitive and made our public figures guarded and jumpy for fear of having a "gotcha" moment. The irony is that the general public feeds on these moments like sharks looking for blood and then turns around and complains about lack of access or calls the current focus of attention antisocial and elitist for not mingling with the general public.

I am not giving these public officials a pass because, especially in regard to elected Democrats, I feel like most of the time I have the opportunity to play Whac-A-Mole. But let's be realistic. How many times in a day do you do something stupid or say something that makes no sense and you instantly realize it? Now, how would you feel if every mistake you made every day had the potential of being the lead story on a newscast or the headline of the morning paper? Talk about enough motivation for anyone to become a recluse!

Our Founding Fathers believed so much in the freedom of speech and the freedom of the press that they made sure to put them in the First Amendment. They had seen what happened when a government controlled the opinions and information that was being released to the general public. They did not want America to share in the same fate. However, when James Madison wrote the Bill of Rights, I guarantee he believed the majority of citizens would have the motivation to only speak the truth and promote this new country in a positive manner since they had the images of sacrificed blood still etched in their minds.

Our Founding Fathers could never have imagined things like the World Wide Web, Twitter, live streaming or texting. They could not imagine the concept of information getting to people as soon as an event was occurring. Just as with the Second Amendment, our Bill of Rights does not come with bullet points; it is left to the people to be responsible and make judgments for themselves.

Taking Up the Mantle

More importantly the mantle to set the example for these new forms of journalism is on the shoulders of the established media and I applaud Attkisson, Wahl, and any other journalists in the field who choose their integrity and reputation over a coveted position and paycheck.

This might be my Jerry Maguire moment. Remember at the beginning of the classic romantic movie, where Tom Cruise's character spends an entire night writing what he later terms a mission statement, titled, "The Things We Think and Do Not Say"? I believe everyone at some point has this moment in life when they have their own epiphany about their life and their surroundings. This chapter just might be mine . . . where I pour my heart and soul into a manifesto of journalistic definition and the importance of integrity.

Journalist, do not choose this field because you are looking for a nine-to-five job with great benefits. I believe true journalists don't have a choice in their life's work because there is no separation between our personal and professional lives. Every action we take, we're looking for the story . . . whether we're pumping gas and analyzing why the prices are rising or falling, or we're playing at the park and taking note of what our friends are chatting about. I believe a journalist is someone who has a passion for the story whether that story is filled with facts, opinions, or mixed with both. It doesn't matter whether or not you tell the story in words or images, via television, online, radio, or a mix of all of those.

True journalists love the news and more importantly love the country and the people whom they are talking about. We want our stories to produce results that make our world a better place and want to be remembered as a person whose work could be trusted to be of integrity, respect, and meaning.

As individuals within the movement continue to realize their own power to change opinion, we will hopefully see more start to express their Conservative political opinion in public. It is hopeful that like a snowball, once a single voice is heard, and others who are silent realize they are not alone in their beliefs, they will also speak their opinion. In fact, thanks to technology, the Conservative movement has the opportunity today to be stronger than ever. We will find we are not the minority opinion in America, which is what the ongoing goal of the Progressives has been until now. By keeping us silent, they have kept us in isolation.

It's amazing how just taking a minute from your day to update your status or tweet your opinion on an issue can influence and inform others. Just like an animal seeing the light of day for the first time, the feeling of knowing that you are potentially making a difference and changing the opinion of just one uninformed or misinformed voter is empowering. Whether it is your best friend from high school or a stranger you never met before, you now hold the power to be a catalyst, someone who takes a small issue to the forefront of the Conservative movement and ultimately affects the outcome of a campaign or issue.

CHAPTER SEVEN

Religious Freedom for Tigers, Nuns, and Hobby Lobby

RECENTLY IN SOUTH Carolina, the coach of the very popular Clemson Tigers football team was under fire for preaching his faith inappropriately—and as expected, the flame-throwing Progressives quickly screamed that he had violated an imaginary constitutional mandate stating that church and state remain distant from one another. If we want to discuss the issue of the relationship between church and state, this anecdote from the Southern half of the United States is a good place to start; the story pretty much covers everything wrong with the Progressive attacks on religious groups and communities that wish to publicly display or avow their beliefs in their own communities, which—and keep this in mind—is a very different thing than forcing others to ascribe to those particular sets of beliefs.

Recently a friend of mine, when I told him about writing this particular chapter, asked if I would have a problem with, say, a Muslim community displaying a statue of the Koran in a municipal building. And I have to say—acknowledging of course that we do actually face a threat from homegrown terrorists in this country, and that should never be taken lightly—if the community was predominately Muslim, I don't see much of a problem with that. The great thing about freedom is that no one can make you believe—or even make you say you believe—in something without your consent, and the existence of a statue doesn't change that. USA! USA!

But the militant atheists seem to have trouble understanding this concept. And the story out of Clemson, South Carolina, illustrates it.

What It Does Say . . . and What It Doesn't

So what happened is this: The Freedom from Religion Foundation (FFRF)—a charming little atheist group based in Madison, Wisconsin, that sends out requests via its website for "godless quotes of the day"—has charged Clemson Tigers' head football coach Dabo Swinney with "unconstitutional behavior," and went so far as to send a letter to the public university as a kind of formal complaint. (They clearly feel the threat of those crazy religious types some nine hundred miles away.)

Now, never mind that no one actually complained to the FFRF about Swinney's activities, which included prayers before games, the hiring of a team chaplain, and team devotionals. In fact, the FFRF just decided one day, out of the blue apparently, to target a public university in the buckle of the Southern Baptist Bible Belt for doing what almost every other school in the South does, both public and private. The atheists in Wisconsin, in the absence of a first-person complaint, filed an open-records request and found evidence of Fellowship of Christian Athletes meetings and other such horrific get-togethers, so they decided something must be done. Because the republic was in danger. Or something.

The whole thing bears the mark of an actual, honest-to-God witch hunt, something we used to find distasteful in this country. But the attention nonetheless led the coach and the team to have to defend themselves on the national stage because of the separation of church and state, y'all.

Now, just bear with me because in some cases this concept can work in our favor. But here's where Progressives ruin everything, as they so often do.

Did you know that the term "separation of church and state" never appears in the actual Constitution? That's a true story. The First Amendment is the part of the Constitution people mean when they talk about church and state, and it very clearly reads:

> Congress shall make no law respecting an establishment of religion, or prohibiting the free exercise thereof.

To translate from the funky sentence construction of the eighteenth century, what this means is that no law will be made by Congress with regard to religion (i.e., there will be no state religion and there will be no favoritism of one religion over any other). That's what's known as the "establishment clause." The second part, "the free-exercise clause," was intended to do just what it says: protect the people as they worship in the way they see fit. That doesn't mean, of course, that you can engage in honor killings in the name of religion. Rather, if religious practices don't interfere with another person's civil liberties, they are protected under this provision of the Constitution.

One of the worst misunderstandings of this clause today is that it was designed to protect government from religion. In fact, it's just the opposite: it was designed to protect religion from government interference. The reason we know this is because the Founders were explicitly clear that they wanted to avoid the problems they had left behind in Europe, many of them resulting from the fusion of the state with the religion of the day. And, as we try to remember every Thanksgiving, the first people to hit our shores were looking to worship without having the state breathing down their necks and executing them for not practicing the sanctioned religion.

Did this mean that the Founders and framers of our original documents wanted to pretend people didn't still care about freedom of worship now that they were part of a new nation being forged from some ragtag British colonies? Well, that would just be stupid. And those guys were anything but.

So, given that there's nothing in the actual Constitution using the phrase "separation of church and state," where do we get the phrase? It's clear that the Founders didn't expect that church and state were to be considered operating as separate entities per se. Rather, Congress was not to start passing legislation that favored one religion over another and most *certainly* not to be telling people they couldn't worship in the ways and manners they chose (excepting, of course, when it's kooky and weird and trampling over other people's rights to free expression or life, liberty, and the pursuit of happiness, etc.).

This is why most of us conservative Christians are stuck with the shallow end of the gene poolers like the mouthbreathers at Westboro Baptist Church. Even though their leader, Fred Phelps, has passed away and many family and church members have left the congregation, others there continue to carry on the despicable actions they claim are done in God's name. I don't like what they say or do, but the establishment clause and the free expression clause of the First Amendment prohibit the federal government from silencing them.

And really, we shouldn't want it any other way.

To reiterate, this does not mean that our Founders considered religion divorced from the state. Moreover—and this is more timely—it does not mean they had the idea that no one should ever exhibit anything religious at any time, lest some other religion gets antsy and feels slighted or left out. It simply means that centralized power—in, say, a state religion—was as dangerous a concept to those great men as centralized power was in one branch of government, or under one tyrannical man. As *Forbes* contributor Bill Flax put it in his piece "The True Meaning of Separation of Church and State":

> Thus the Constitution decreed that Washington had no occasion or authority to interject itself into matters as obviously local as doctrines of faith. Congress was not empowered to establish a church because the framers feared that concentrated power, whether favored religions, standing armies, banking monopolies, or an overarching federal government, invited tyranny.
>
> Church and state were distinct in that the Federal Government could not elevate one denomination over others. Nor could government and its flawed inhabitants usurp divine authority by harnessing politics to the church. Faith is no civil contract, but a personal matter not to be profaned by politics.[10]

"A personal matter not to be profaned by politics." That's a great statement, which I think frames the most important reason people freak out about *any* religious mention of *any* kind—be it prayer in schools, an effigy of the Ten Commandments in a municipal building, or prayer before a high-school sporting event. What that statement means, in a general sense, is that the church should be protected from the state, not that the state be protected from the church. Those wise men who wrote our founding documents had a healthy respect for moral and religious teaching as well as a healthy respect for the Enlightenment belief that all ideas and convictions at least be considered. Thomas Jefferson is the one who coined the phrase "a wall of separation" between church and state.

Those wise men who wrote our founding documents had a healthy respect for moral and religious teaching as well as a healthy respect for the Enlightenment belief that all ideas and convictions at least be considered.

As I mentioned at the beginning of this chapter, many think these words are actually contained within the Constitution. In fact, Jefferson was responding to a church that was concerned that there would be one state religion and that they would be left out in the cold regarding preferential treatment for one religion over another. So he was assuaging their fears. Again, this was by no means an attempt by Jefferson to assert that religious conviction was separate from governing in the burgeoning new country just finding its feet. Many, many years later, another president—Ronald Reagan— understood the proper balance when he said, "We establish no religion in this country, we command no worship, we mandate no belief, nor will we ever. Church and state are, and must remain, separate. All are free to believe or not believe, all are free to practice a faith or not, and those who believe are free, and should be free, to speak of and act on their belief."

How Did We Wind Up Here?

So how did we go from the idea that "freedom of religious expression should be guaranteed at the highest levels of government" to one that says we are not to express our religious beliefs publicly in any quasi-governmental building or in any capacity that may appear to be sanctioned, or funded, by taxpayer money? Does the establishment clause really mandate that a concrete version of the Ten Commandments—or the Koran or the Torah or any other overtly religious text—be hidden from view in public buildings? And is the Clemson football coach really breaking some kind of law to hire a chaplain to lead prayers for his team before it takes the field?

Well, we can thank Thomas Jefferson for giving us this great quote:

> The legitimate powers of government extend to such acts only as are injurious to others. But it does me no injury for my neighbor to say there are twenty gods, or no god. It neither picks my pocket nor breaks my leg.[11]

Jefferson was alluding to the idea that there are issues that affect freedom—infringing on freedom and the aforementioned life, liberty, and the pursuit of happiness thing—that are more compelling and more deleterious than a disagreement over religious beliefs. And those are the things the government should concern itself with, not how, when, and in what manner a group chooses to commune with God. And my guess is that Jefferson would have been horrified with the FFRF invoking the Constitution to try to prevent a group from worshiping as it saw fit. Because that's actually the opposite of what the establishment and the free exercise clauses were designed to do, which was to protect a group like the Clemson team so people could worship as they saw fit. But the FFRF must not believe in the rule of law either.

There have been some rather unconstitutional things happening regarding this concept of a separate church and state, but they're not coming out of state universities or municipal buildings across the country. Nope, they're coming right out of the halls of Congress and the White House, and they have everything to do with mandating that a group of people stop worshiping in the manner their religious affiliation dictates (just like at Clemson) so they can jump on board the great boondoggle of a wealth redistribution scheme you may know as Obamacare.

Consider the case recently heard by the Supreme Court where the private business Hobby Lobby sued for the right to refuse providing certain kinds of birth control they consider tantamount to abortion pills through their employee health insurance, even though Obamacare has demanded they do

so. ("Congress shall make no law respecting an establishment
of religion, or prohibiting the free exercise thereof"? Yeah,
right!) Or what about the Catholic colleges rejecting the same
mandate on similar grounds? Add to that the ongoing story
brought up about eight years ago of the IRS threatening religious leaders who discuss politics from their pulpits and
frame it in today's terms, all while the IRS is basically threatening anybody who disagrees with the current Progressive
ideology, which continues to do great damage to our once
great republic. From the *Wall Street Journal*, we read:

> Earlier this year, 31 Ohio pastors called down the
> most powerful force they could find against two
> of their fellow church leaders in Columbus. No, it
> wasn't God—but close.
>
> In a complaint filed with the Internal Revenue
> Service, the pastors alleged that the Rev. Russell
> Johnson and the Rev. Rod Parsley crossed the line
> into advocacy over the past year by preaching on
> political topics . . .
>
> Just a few weeks after the pastors filed their
> grievance, the IRS released a report on the outcome
> of 132 similar anonymous filings against nonprofit
> organizations during the course of the 2004 pres-
> idential campaign, 63 of which are churches. The
> allegations against the churches include: inviting
> candidates to speak, donating money to politicians,

endorsing individual candidates and publishing voter guides. Some of the cases were thrown out immediately, but 37 of the 47 churches that were investigated further were deemed to have run afoul of the tax code.[12]

The Founders would be horrified if they were around today and could see for themselves that their noble idea of keeping the government's untrustworthy fingers out of the people's right to worship has been so corrupted that it has now become a tool by the government to tell people what they must do.

THE FOUNDERS WOULD be horrified if they were around today and could see for themselves that their noble idea of keeping the government's untrustworthy fingers out of the people's right to worship has been so corrupted.

They would be equally horrified to hear of something like what happened recently in Ohio:

A group advocating the separation of church and state is protesting a pair of crosses displayed for Easter on a tiny eastern Ohio village's municipal building . . .

Mayor John Abdalla temporarily removed the crosses in January after the foundation threatened to sue, but he returned them to celebrate the Easter season. One is Latin, the other Eastern Orthodox.

Abdalla told the Steubenville Herald-Star that such seasonal displays were allowed . . .

He told the newspaper he planned to remove them at the end of April.[13]

In the world of Benjamin Franklin, George Washington, and Thomas Jefferson, this kind of overzealous policing of religious practices by a community would have been an affront to the prescribed role of government. Bear in mind again that a mysteriously named "group representing separation of church and state" were the ones who contacted the mayor and complained, just like what happened in the Clemson case. What makes this important is that it's not people in the community itself who have an issue with the religious display around an overtly Christian holiday, for they are not the ones who filed a complaint. No, it's some third-party group that takes it upon itself to be offended and outraged on behalf of the rest of us. Chances are that mysterious group isn't based in that community, maybe not even in the state of Ohio. So how they can possibly be offended is something of a brainteaser. And yet they get to badger and threaten and stomp around like bullies telling everyone else what they should do.

C. S. Lewis, the great Christian apologist, perhaps said it best when he pointed out that this bureaucratic morality pushing from our government—because they do react to the bullies in today's Progressive climate—is nothing less than a tyranny:

> Of all tyrannies, a tyranny sincerely exercised for the good of its victims may be the most oppressive. It may be better to live under robber barons than under omnipotent moral busybodies. The robber baron's cruelty may sometimes sleep, his cupidity may at some point be satiated; but those who torment us for our own good will torment us without end, for they do so with the approval of their own conscience.[14]

And our Founders were, if nothing else, adamantly opposed to tyranny in all its forms. They waged a war of independence over it, for goodness sake. And yet, a few generations later, here we are, turning back their work by allowing a Big Brother government to go into quiet communities and bully them about their crosses on Easter. This seems to be the opposite of looking to a king and saying, "Hey there, we don't want to be ruled by you. You can't come into our colonies and start dictating what we think. We don't want to be Anglicans and worship the Church of England and the crown."

But it's happening.

Religious Freedom in Health Care

So, if Obamacare is the real constitutional threat, what kind of chance do we have to make sure that Congress doesn't make this mistake with other grand pieces of legislation that begin to infringe on our basic rights to be left alone to talk to God within our individual communities as we please? Because even though Obamacare contains a religious exemption, it's apparently extremely difficult to get your hands on it, as reported by the *Washington Post*:

> Nestled in the fine print of the Affordable Care Act is a clause that allows people of certain religions to seek an exemption from the requirement to carry health insurance or pay a fine.
>
> The clause applies only to denominations that run their own "mutual aid" system of spreading the cost of health care across the community.
>
> That's how the Amish, and to a lesser extent Mennonites, traditionally handled health expenses.[15]

On a community level, that "mutual aid" system is pretty close to being something like a cost redistribution scheme, and it's clever of the *Washington Post* to remind us that those groups that were escaping religious persecution like the Amish and the Mennonites, that's how they do things. Haters.

Except, things that work on a community level can't always be blown out to work on a national and federal level. The precursor to Obamacare—Romneycare in Massachusetts—proved that. It wasn't a total disaster on a smaller scale, primarily because the goal wasn't to use the nobler ideas behind it—namely that "mutual aid" thing—as a way to massively collect and then redistribute the wealth in a way that would have made Marx turn cartwheels in his furry little hat.

The Amish and the Mennonite communities are small and have established a way to insulate themselves from the larger world by being something of a commune. It works for them because they are not actually trying to steal from each other. Rather, they are trying to help each other, in good Christian fashion.

However, the creators and pushers of Obamacare—and their mouthpieces at the *Washington Post*—are trying to steal from those who sign up as well as from the taxpayers who fund the program so they can provide the most basic and crummiest health insurance they can, all the while reaping the benefits of the need for funding to maintain it. It's all a giant scam. And there's a reason it doesn't work; if it worked, there would be no reason to throw more money at it to fix it.

Add to that this idea that religious groups and leaders, and even those who just resist based on the pull of their own conscience, are being told that they are forbidden from opting out. One of the most—*evil?* yeah, let's call it evil—evil things attached to Obamacare was the notion that you were mandated by law to buy health insurance, and if you couldn't, you were ordered to pay a fine. So either way, you were giving some of your money to Uncle Sam. And if you didn't care for the morning-after drugs that were covered under the most basic plans you were required to buy because your heart and soul told you that life begins at conception, well, who are you to stop the brilliant system that was ensuring everyone would be covered? You must be a bad person to want to do that. Wanting to stop the systematic destruction of life makes you a bad person in the world of Obamacare.

It's now even so bad that our own president—who, by the way, really apparently hates that his name is attached to this monstrosity of law—has taken to mocking the Catholic nuns who are uncomfortable with Obamacare's contraception mandate.

Judge Napolitano, in an op-ed piece for the *Washington Times,* wrote:

> When the Framers were putting together the Constitution in Philadelphia in the summer of 1787, they knew the states would not adopt it without written guarantees that the new central government would respect natural rights, . . .
>
> One of those rights guarantees the free exercise of religion . . .
>
> [Obama's] Department of (political) Justice has vigorously resisted the nuns [who oppose Obamacare] and even mocked them. It has demanded that they assert in writing what their religious beliefs are and that they permit others to

pay for the contraceptive, sterilization and abortion services they do not want, cannot use and profoundly condemn.

Our post-Obamacare world is dangerous for people informed by conscience and presupposing respect for natural rights . . .

If the government can tax you and me and selfless nuns for fidelity to long-held religious beliefs while exempting others because of their fleeting political beliefs, then the Free Exercise Clause of the First Amendment is meaningless. Our rights are in the hands of a congressionally enabled tyrant.[16]

Reminiscent of that C. S. Lewis quote. And it has gotten just that bad. The US Catholic Bishops asserting in 2013 that they were adamantly opposed to the contraception mandate in Obamacare, even stated that they would be willing to go to jail for their beliefs, because that's sort of how religiously convicted people roll. Their standards are nonnegotiable and they are willing to suffer whatever consequences may come from standing by their principles. Not so the Obamacare pushers, who have backtracked and mandated and changed their minds three hundred times when facing any pushback from the public as they learn more and more the truths about this "law of the land" that was sold to them in a shiny body, but had the engine of a lemon under the hood.

Where We Are Today

So where does it all stand now? Well, the Hobby Lobby case, which was recently heard by the Supreme Court, should be an interesting standard-bearer of things to come. Hobby Lobby and a company called Conestoga Wood were both suing former Health and Human Services Director Kathleen Sebelius.

> Hobby Lobby contends its "religious beliefs prohibit them from providing health coverage for contraceptive drugs and devices that end human life after conception." The question these cases are seeking to solve is whether for-profit companies have a right to exercise religious freedom under the Religious Freedom Restoration Act . . . that states the "Government shall not substantially burden a person's exercise of religion even if the burden results from a rule of general applicability."[17]

Hobby Lobby didn't have a problem with providing contraception; their issue was with providing *emergency* contraception (i.e., morning-after pills, etc.) because they believe that these are basically the same thing as abortions in a bottle (my words). When conception occurs and you take one of these things, make no mistake . . . they cause you to abort that rapidly dividing little cell. So, Hobby Lobby and Conestoga were being pretty reasonable. They just didn't want to sign onto providing a form of birth control because it violates their consciences to do so—and they were forced to defend that conviction in front of the Supreme Court. I'm sure that if Thomas Jefferson could have witnessed this playing out, his powdered wig would have caused quite a cloud as he jumped up and down in protest. Can you imagine? The man who said the government should not be allowed to dictate how a religious group is allowed to worship would be appalled that a religious conviction must be defended before the government in such a manner.

But our constitutional lawyer president doesn't see it that way, I guess.

The Obama administration argues that it's a woman's right to have the freedom to choose her own health coverage. The other side is crying foul because of the violation of religious freedoms guaranteed by the Constitution, the defining law of the land at the inception of the country.

It should be a no-brainer, right? It should never have come before the Supreme Court, right? Rational and logical people recognize that, yes. No doubt our Founding Fathers would have recognized this as well. But apparently not Kathleen Sebelius or Barack Obama or the entire cadre of Democratic senators and members of Congress who voted to let this hideous miscarriage of law pass and be foisted upon an unsuspecting people who were just hoping to maybe have to pay less in insurance (but that, too, was a big fat lie).

Luckily, in this case the Supreme Court ruled in favor of Hobby Lobby. Their fight against the Affordable Health Care Act's individual mandate was based on the concept of the craft store operating "in a manner consistent with Biblical principals."

"It's been a long journey, but an important one for our family and for those who wish to be guided in all areas of life, including their businesses by faith and conscience," Hobby Lobby co-founder Barbara Green said in a statement after the ruling.

While this was a huge victory for the religious right regarding whether the government can force business owners to act against their faith, this doesn't strike a death blow to Obamacare, although it might be the first stab at what could eventually become fatal. But as with anything in our movement, we thrive on momentum. It often takes just a small victory to energize our batteries so we can keep fighting until the next victory is achieved . . . and so on.

So here we have just two examples of how the government and religious institutions and activities are intersecting one another. One has mysterious and agenda-driven outside groups grousing because people are praying on a football field. The other is mocking nuns and requiring reasonable people who object to one small provision of a gargantuan money-grab fighting for their lives and their souls before the highest court in the land—not to mention being called all kinds of distasteful things in the media by the mouthpieces of progressivism.

It does make one wonder: what would Thomas Jefferson and other framers of our Constitution think of this mess?

CHAPTER EIGHT

Women in Combat (and I Don't Mean Black Friday)

G ONE ARE THE days when women were generally happy in their traditional roles as women and men were happy in their traditional roles as men. Times when we all raised our kids with traditional values also seem to be slipping away. Instead, they have been replaced by a media rich with negativity, violence, and Liberal ideals. We now live in a society where men marry men, women marry women, and if you are born a gender you don't want to be you can just change it. Feminist women have continued to fight for equality well beyond the point of reason.

I am a huge advocate of women's strength and place in society, and I strongly encourage them to use their voices both politically and socially to take a stand for what they believe.

I want them to stand toe-to-toe with men during intellectual conversations and in corporate environments.

However, I draw the line when it comes to women in combat. This is not a place for women. The irony of it all is that while the mass media and Liberal activists are busy condemning gun ownership and persecuting little boys for playing with toy guns, they have been leading a fight to put women on the front lines of war. And I am not talking about some figurative front lines—literally, the place where there are tanks, bombs, trenches, barbwire, and bullets. A thought which is just plain ridiculous. They are fighting to go against everything natural about gender roles.

Unfortunately, as a result of activists' push, in January 2013 our government removed the ban on women serving in combat. This is a huge mistake! Additionally, military leadership has asked for updated draft regulations, which would include both men and women. While they work on figuring out plans and timelines on how best to integrate women into these roles, mothers across the country now worry, Will my daughter have to register for a draft? Will this be the next phase in the quest for ultimate gender equality?

A Mother's Perspective

Personally, it's a thought I can't even stomach. As the mother of both a son and a daughter, this is certainly a thought I had about him . . . but never her! I am very proud of my husband, who served in the Army prior to our meeting; however,

I don't know if I could handle the stress and worry of being married to someone deployed. I am not afraid to admit that I have called just to see if he was okay when a traffic accident alert pops up on my phone; I know that I would probably need to be sedated if he was ever deployed. The only pain worse than that would be to be the mother of a son in direct combat, much less a daughter!

My mind swirls with all the possibilities, and I worry. There is no way I could ever prepare my daughter for this situation. What can I do to protect her? Raising a daughter is tricky enough these days, and my job as a mother just became more difficult. Not only do I have to worry about mean girls on the playground, dates to the dance, or the price tag of the latest fashion, but now I have to worry about the idea that if there ever is a national draft again, my daughter might get the opportunity to sit in a foxhole wet, cold, and muddy, holding a tactical assault rifle in her rough, cracked, chapped hands, waiting to kill or be killed, or something even worse . . . captured, raped, and tortured.

Despite society's trend to the contrary, Chris and I are raising our children with traditional values. We want our son to be a gentleman and our daughter to be a lady. We won't accept anything less. For my son, this includes protecting women, being kind to them, letting them go first, and never ever hitting a girl. Collectively, we as mothers should want our sons to be this way. We should want them to practice chivalry and treat women appropriately. This concept plays right into God's idea for roles between men and women. I am not going to lie . . . raising them this way is difficult. More and more media, movies, games, and other cultural influences are including and portraying nontraditional values. Nonetheless, it's my goal as a mother to make sure my children know and understand the godly roles they are to play here on earth.

With women serving in combat roles, how are we to explain to our sons as they enter the military that to survive, they will need to reject all those gentlemanly things we taught them? Oh, but then remember to pick them back up when you return home and try to have a family. Geez. How confusing!

WITH WOMEN SERVING in combat roles, how are we to explain to our sons as they enter the military that to survive, they will need to reject all those gentlemanly things we taught them?

Knowing my son already has his eyes on a military career, this frightens me. It's our goal to prepare our children for what life may have in store and to give them the skills and knowledge necessary to handle all situations—happy, disappointing, or dangerous. That being said, with new military changes on the horizon, I wonder if I should prepare my son for how difficult a military career may now be. Should I alter the way I am teaching him to view women? Even if I decide not to, will other parents join the trends? As if video games aren't already too violent, will the next military game include women being mistreated, tortured, and killed while fighting in combat? What about my sweet daughter? What do I need to do to prepare her for what may come?

G. I. Joe and G. I. Jane

Why must some women, these female combat activists, push so hard for total equality in the military? It's not like there are not plenty of other places these women can serve if they feel the need to fulfill their patriotic calling. Currently, the U.S. military has around 215,000 women serving in active duty, which is close to 15 percent of the total military enlistments. The National Guard and the Reserves boast a little higher with about 119,000 (20 percent) Reservists and 470,000 (15.5 percent) in the National Guard.[18] These are women who serve in various roles, and without them our military would be weakened. Women's involvement in the military is a great legacy of strength and courage during difficult times. Those who continue to push for women in combat make a mockery of all they accomplished and discount their previous roles. It is also extremely disrespectful to the men who have served and currently serve in these combat positions.

I realize there are many who do not share my opinion. Comedian Elayne Boosler jokes, "We have women in the military, but they don't put us in the front lines. They don't know if we can fight, if we can kill. I think we can. All the general has to do is walk over to the women and say, 'You see the

enemy over there? They say you look fat in those uniforms.'"
Seriously, though, many folks think we should just let those
who want to serve do so. I mean, what's the difference, right?
To each their own, so to speak.

Well, that's not the case. If letting a few dedicated, hard-
core women who are out to prove something leads to a fe-
male-registered draft, then it does affect me! I can't stand by
and let this happen. I can't allow my daughter to be forced into
a horror she could never imagine. And yes, I did say *horror*.

Combat is nasty. Men on the front lines see, hear, and
do things that would make most people cringe at the mere
thought. There has always been an important role for women
in the military, and I don't think there is one person in
America who thinks women should not be able to serve in
some capacity. The problem comes with this new generation
of feminists who want women to fight shoulder to shoulder
on the front lines of combat with men and are either unrealistic or too ignorant to think that their presence won't have
any affect.

Now I know that Demi Moore's character in the movie
G.I. Jane kicked some serious tail. I also admit that many of
us joke with our spouses or friends that we are just as tough
as they are, and in many ways we probably are. However, the
problem is that we *are* different. We are built differently and
are designed by God both physically and mentally to be different. Whether the feminists want to admit it or not, we have
different roles to fulfill here on earth. It is what it is. Female

bodies were designed to carry babies. They are supposed to be softer, fuller, subtle—not hard, toughened killing machines. Female muscles and body strength are different from that of males.

Men by nature are stronger and can push their bodies to extremes. God designed them to be our protectors. This is evident when evaluating the physical fitness standards for the US Army and US Marine Corps. Both have gaps in expectations on performance tests for males versus females. Women are not even required to do pull-ups for the USMC Initial Strength Test or the Physical Fitness Test, and the maximum female run time in the Army is equivalent to the minimum allowed for some males to pass.[19]

These are just a couple of examples of reasons women physically can't measure up to their male counterparts on the front lines. Would I worry if my husband's life depended on a female comrade to drag his 230 pounds to safety? Absolutely! And if you ask him, he would too! As much as the female combat activists want to fight it, they just can't measure up physically.

In truth, I am not sure how they can truly call it "equal" when in fact the testing standards aren't themselves equal between the two genders.

Then you add the mental aspect. Women have hormones. They are those crazy things that fluctuate on any given basis at any age, with little or no warning. How do they plan to control those? I can barely handle mine while watching a commercial that tugs at my heartstrings. How will they deal with seeing the horrors of war, sitting next to men in foxholes, and firing back at armed children? These are the realities of war, and I just don't think women were designed to handle those types of situations. Activists are so busy fighting for the point, they aren't stopping to think of the actual realities of what they are asking for or the impact it might have on all women, not just those who are crazy enough to think they belong on the front lines!

ACTIVISTS ARE SO busy fighting for the point, they aren't stopping to think of the actual realities of what they are asking for or the impact it might have on all women.

Other Considerations

In one episode of *The Office*, Angela dated and slept with Andy, then cheated on him with Dwight, then broke up with Andy for Dwight, then broke up with Dwight for another man, whom she then cheated on with Dwight too. This was certainly awkward to watch, mostly because things like that unfortunately do occur in real life. Workplace relationships and love triangles do happen. Can you imagine a similar situation in the field of combat where life and death is on the line and one soldier can't quit thinking about his female comrade who last week was his girlfriend but this week is dating another guy in his platoon? Just as it happens among civilians, it will happen with women in combat. If anything, the possibility for trouble may be heightened due to the overwhelming stress and emotions involved on the battlefield.

Men in the military have talked for years about "Jody," the given name to any man at home who is moving in on a deployed soldier's woman. They often tease each other about "Jody" as a way to bring laughter to a real issue they worry about. How complicated would this be if their significant other was on deployment as well and "Jody" was an actual longtime buddy. "Workplace romances" are not only difficult for those involved but are also very awkward for coworkers. These relationships would certainly cause some issues and could easily be a threat to the safety and security of the mission as well as to fellow soldiers.

Or on the flip side of this, what if a wife is at home during her husband's deployment and, along with other more common concerns, she now has to worry about sexual relationships forming between her husband and another woman who are in combat together? When you take people out of their normal environment and thrust them into real life-and-death situations, it has an effect on emotions and decisions. I have heard stories over and over about soldiers who find ways to cheat while on deployment. The numbers will only go up as the opportunity to cheat increases and is put right in their faces every day.

Going one step further, we have to admit that many of these combat relationships will result in pregnancy, which may go undetected for a while in a combat environment. Fabulous! Typically, by instinct and just the way nature designed it, these women would require the ultimate need for protection. It's an issue that can put the unit in jeopardy whether they stay or go home. If they stay, the issue is obvious; if they go, the unit loses a person they have trained with and depended on.

What kind of prenatal care would they get while in combat? How would the men left behind feel about the situation? I can guarantee it would affect them. What about those who conceive just before deployment? The same situation would happen to them. How long till they realize? Will they be sent home? Currently women who are pregnant are nondeployable. It's a well-known fact that many female servicewomen purposely become pregnant to avoid deployment. Well. how about that? I can only imagine these numbers will rise.

Talk about equality with exceptions! It seems like they want to pick and choose when they want equal rights. I can assure you that no serviceman has been able to avoid deployment because his wife was pregnant. In fact, many servicemen don't even get leave when their wives are due for delivery. They miss precious moments and bonding time with their children, often meeting them for the first time as a stranger when they are many months old. How is this fair and equal?

This is another great example of how they argue for equality—saying male and female can both do the same, yet the females are given different standards. It certainly can't be because mothers and fathers aren't equally important in raising children. It's because women's role on earth is to have babies and to nurture and feed them in their early stages, while a father's role is to provide and protect during these times. It's amazing how the current administration picks and chooses which concepts they want to include in their ideology.

What about the nonconsensual sexual relations? Rape. It's a horrible act. There is no excuse for it whatsoever. However, there are a few issues I want to point out. When I was growing up, my parents repeatedly told me to "avoid situations" that would put me in places I didn't want to be. I would hear it each time I left the house to go out on my own. It was that subtle reminder from my dad to be careful whom I was with and where I was at all times. This concept became my inner protection. Naturally, as a result of this conditioning, I could never imagine being the sole woman or even one of a few women within a large group of highly charged men. Not a place I would feel safe. This isn't a knock on those men; I am just saying the situation is already staged with potential problems. What are the women thinking? Military sexual assault statistics are already on the rise and seem to get higher each year.

During the military fiscal year 2013, the number of sexual assaults reported was 5,061, a 50-percent increase from the previous year.[20] What do they think will happen when you thrust women into the most tumultuous situations the military has to offer? We ask these men to tap into a side most civilized men don't even have. They have to be able to set aside certain emotions to accomplish the job. Even from the earliest stages, military members are subject to mental conditioning in addition to their physical training. This conditioning is supposed to help them handle the intense situations they face during conflict. I have even heard the behavior described as "animalistic" when they go through training to basically become killing machines when needed.

These same men are supposed to be able to fully control themselves around women. As much as we would love to think this is possible, for many it is not because it's very difficult to just flip the switch back and forth as required. The result is unnecessary violence, including rape. Let's don't forget aggressive women also. Some women, particularly those who crave power, are often aggressive with men. They can be very pushy. If they get their mind set on something or someone, they will not be easily derailed from their pursuit. This possibility would certainly be unsettling for a wife at home. And let's not forget that in some of these cases, men are the victims. The percentages may be smaller, but they still exist nonetheless.

Perhaps the government should spend time focusing on ways to resolve the current issues within the military before introducing new conflicts. These rush decisions only will add fuel to a fire already smoldering. I shudder to think what the sexual assault statistics will be in a few years. And this is just within our own ranks. We haven't even talked about what will happen to them as prisoners of war.

So what about when female infantry soldiers become POWs? They are beaten, raped, tortured. This is definitely not something any parent would want to happen to their children, especially their daughters. How about being beaten to death and dragged through the streets half naked as combatants did with servicemen in Somalia? What if they were among the servicemen killed by terrorists and hanged from a bridge in Iraq? Or forced to live in solitary confinement, crammed within small boxes or "tiger cages," as POWs had to endure in Vietnam? The next terrorist video could show a female POW blindfolded and about to be beheaded. It is crazy to think, but certainly possible as more and more of them show up in direct combat in war zones. How would the world respond to seeing these images? What kind of emotional effect will it have on our daughters who may have to sign up for a draft in the future?

Women have always been viewed differently in society. Remember the sinking *Titanic*? Women and children were the first evacuated off the boat. For centuries, women and children have been the first saved in emergencies and offered exclusion and sanctuary during conflict, basically considered untouchable by all ethical standards . . . until now. Having females suddenly show up in the front lines on battlefields will certainly disrupt this normal and traditional way of life. This change in thought process could also eventually affect how civilian women are treated during conflict by enemies, as they would no longer being treated in a protected and respectful manner. The administration and the activists clearly have no idea what series of events could unfold as a result of their decision to lift the ban.

President Obama's ideology of allowing women in combat truly ignores many of the international traditions within the Middle Eastern countries in which we have been fighting over the past two decades. As if this president's foreign policy hasn't had enough problems! I can only imagine how the implementation of these new policies will affect relationships with both our allies and our enemies. How will this new policy work in ally nations whose national religion is Muslim?

PRESIDENT OBAMA'S IDEOLOGY of allowing women in combat truly ignores many of the international traditions within the Middle Eastern countries in which we have been fighting over the past two decades.

Do you really think these countries will allow women to fight alongside their soldiers? Will our ladies have to wear burkas in respect to their culture? I cannot imagine American women running across the desert, M-16 shouldered, and a ninety-pound pack on their back, robes flapping. Yes, that's a ridiculous (and hopefully unlikely) absurd picture, but seriously, how are we supposed to gain respect and trust from our allies when we force them to fight alongside women, whom they culturally disrespect? What about our Muslim enemies and terrorists? How will they react to having a woman ask them to lay down their weapons? During times when diplomacy is much preferred over more casualties, I don't see any enemy, regardless of culture, being willing to surrender to a woman.

Disrupting the Norm

Ever spent much time around military men when they are with their fellow servicemen? They can be vulgar. The phrase "cuss like a sailor" is very accurate. Imagine an open and honest chat with your girlfriends about men, dating, and marriage, and other personal topics. Now take that and add in a whole bunch of testosterone and a male way of thinking. Stories of sex, women, movies, and more just break the surface of topics these men might cover. After all, what else are they to do when removed from normal life, with nothing to occupy downtime except conversations with friends? Enlisted men laugh and joke and just get downright dirty at times, especially when they are out on their own with no women around. I can't even imagine how stressful combat can be and therefore can understand why men in this environment look for any outlet possible to relax, have a laugh, let some of the stresses go, and bond as a unit.

Most families raise their boys to be respectful around women and to control their language appropriately. This is probably why they feel so free to let go with only their "brothers" around. Naturally, I can imagine some women might be offended by this type of talk and would be upset if exposed to it. Others, as we have seen in the corporate workplace, might even be willing to press charges of sexual harassment just by being exposed to such conversations, particularly a woman who has a chip on her shoulder and is looking to make a point. Having women in the field with these men will totally disrupt unit morale if they are not able to express themselves as they normally would.

While it is hard to believe in an age of rap music, porn on demand, and Miley Cyrus twerking, it is true that the concept of a gentlemen still exists. Just as some women are uncomfortable discussing the details of their monthly cycle around men, I believe most men would be uncomfortable saying certain things in the presence of females. They will always be looking over their shoulder to see who might be listening. On the flip side, say they don't tone it down and the women join them at their level. Will this type of language and behavior become the norm for women? Would it spread beyond the trenches and camps into everyday life at home? Can you imagine the continued disintegration of a society where vulgarity becomes a commonplace and accepted behavior?

Unless you have lived it, you can't understand how these men form relationships with one another that are often closer than family ties. They truly love each other. These tight bonds form as they go through the trenches, suffer, grow, and share together. Throw some estrogen, additional rules, and exceptions into the mix and I have no doubt that these relationships will suffer. Even if the group finds ways to bond and respect the women they serve in combat with, they will never be able to think of them as just "one of the guys." It isn't possible. Why? Because they aren't guys. They are women, with female parts, looks, and thoughts. Men will always see them as more vulnerable and feel the need to shield them. It's just nature. The only way this view would change is to start at birth and try to reculture our boys to think of girls differently. I am just not willing to do that. It goes against everything I believe in.

If we were to institute a draft that included women, not only would this horribly weaken our military, but it would also severely weaken our society. Increased female casualties would limit our country's ability to reproduce and grow. Our country would have women who are mentally ill equipped for the violence and devastation of war heading off to defend the nation. No doubt these women would be trained and prepped for war—and some will most definitely rise to the occasion—however, the majority will not. It's just not natural for women to play this role, and despite all the desensitizing from movies, media, and video games, men will not be able to resist their natural instinct regarding women either. It absolutely will not work.

Then there's the home front. Children could possibly be orphaned from having both parents drafted. What about all the important roles women play at home during war times? Those services would be weakened as well. Throughout history, women have risen to the occasion to help where needed during times of conflict. They take over household duties, raise children, send much-needed supplies to the troops, help keep morale up, and so much more! These jobs are very important. Society could not go on without this much-needed support.

Do you think President Obama has considered his sweet, pampered girls having to register for the draft? I highly doubt it. I am sure he thinks if and when this is implemented, his daughters will somehow be excluded as a result of his power and stature, a mentality likely shared with many of the other activists and politicians who have pushed so hard for the ban to be lifted. Yet again, another exception to their "equality" policies.

Looking Ahead

Many may say, "What's the big deal? We will never have a draft anyway."

Well, we may be closer than you realize. Just look at the fact that it is becoming increasingly harder to recruit a volunteer force and how the president is purposely reducing the number of current enlistees. If a need for war arises, the United States would not be able to fulfill the troop requirements for a large-scale operation.

Meanwhile, there are still possible conflicts on several horizons. Just look at how quickly Al-Qaeda-aligned militants from ISIS—the Islamic State of Iraq and Syria—moved to take over Iraqi cities following President Obama's announced plans for reducing troop numbers in Afghanistan.

During the early stages of the Iraq and Afghanistan wars, military recruiting was down and the wars were quickly expanding. A draft could have been possible, but instead leadership chose to hire contractors, call up reservists, and issue a temporary "stop-loss" to servicemen and servicewomen whose contracts were ending (meaning they were not able to be discharged regardless of their contract end date).

This situation could arise again and they will not have the resources to go with other options. I really don't see the government being able to afford expensive contractors at a similar level should we run into this problem again. They will have no choice but to draft men *and* women should we enter another huge conflict. I mean, hey, I never thought the space program would end, but Obama made that happen. I guess anything is possible under his administration.

What a brave new world my children will grow up in. Am I to raise my daughter to be a soldier while at the same time teaching my son to be man who doesn't put women on a pedestal?

Yes, there was a time when all men in our culture believed women should be on a pedestal and treated accordingly. Thank you, Mr. President, for your Progressive programs to change America into a country that falls in line with your ideology. I fully believe women can do most anything they put their minds to. We have an inner strength that helps us survive the toughest of situations and the ability to be the rock that holds all the pieces together during times of crisis. Trust me, there are enough situations here at home for which we need strong fight-ers. Whether it is your local school board fighting Common Core or your local elected body trying to fight the removal of faith from your city hall, I can assure you there is a place for you to fight passionately within your own community.

There is a vital place for women in the military. We have served in very important roles throughout history and can continue to serve in those roles in the future without jumping into the trenches on the front lines. I have met several strong female soldiers who served in the past or are currently serving who play a very significant role in their divisions. Whether it's as a pilot, part of a medic unit, or as a Public Affairs Officer, there are a plethora of positions where women can serve their country already and are better equipped to do so than their male counterparts.

Shouldn't the commander-in-chief's first priority be to preserve the leading military superpower in the world? Not if your allegiance is to a Progressive doctrine and your asso-ciates and advisors throughout your life have instilled in you an animosity for the US military. With Barack Obama serv-ing at the helm, the Left has a champion of the blame-Amer-ica-first worldview, and a closer look at his defense policies, from military sequestration to gays in the military to women in combat, reveals how openly he has embraced the politics of standing down. The goal is nothing less than eroding the mission and values of the strongest military in the world and forever reducing its capabilities.

Over the last five years, Americans have seen the repeal of the Don't Ask, Don't Tell policy. Obama Pentagon officials have taken the next step of celebrating a homosexual lifestyle within our Armed Forces by hosting events like Gay Pride Day at the Pentagon and initializing gay sensitivity training in the Marine Corps.

Under the umbrella of political correctness, our military was forced to open its arms to radical Islamists who call our military infidels and sworn enemies, for instance in the case of Major Nidal Malik Hasan and the Fort Hood shooting as well as in the case of Fort Campbell's PFC Naser Jason Addo, who was convicted of attempting to use a weapon of mass destruction to blow up a restaurant filled with troops.

Other policies have been put in place to discourage the best from enlisting and becoming commissioned officers. ROTC programs have come under assault at top colleges. Military branches such as the Navy are being told they will be reducing their tuition-assistance programs.

"Sequestration" and the cutting of hundreds of billions of dollars from the defense budget, an idea that was hatched inside the Obama White House, are devastating the military's readiness and morale. Training exercises are being canceled. Ships are being mothballed and aircraft taken out of service.

All of this is happening while our military is being demonized by pop culture. Psy, a Korean music artist whose fame came to him in America for his song "Gangnam Style," released a song promoting the killing of American soldiers.

And well-known rap artist Soulja Boy released a video that included language against our troops too vulgar to be printed in this book.

Hollywood has also done a great job of villainizing our military men and women with the making of movies like *Jarhead, Three Kings,* and the documentary *The Invisible War,* which puts a spotlight on the issue of sexual assault in the military.

The ultimate goal is clear—to neuter America's military as an effective fighting machine and encourage the development of a global "peacekeeping" force. This is in keeping with the Harvard-Bill Ayers-Ivory Tower distrust of, and hostility toward, the American military and preference for a "multipolar" world. The result is an America unable and unwilling to defend its own borders and threats to its people. The war on the military is real. And after eight years with Barack Obama as commander-in-chief, the damage may well prove to be irreversible.

THE ULTIMATE GOAL is clear—to neuter America's military as an effective fighting machine and encourage the development of a global "peacekeeping" force.

Some things are just better left alone and kept the same. Talk to any man who has served and is willing to chat honestly and you will hear more than you ever wanted to know. I have relatives who still struggle talking about things that happened in Vietnam. World War II veterans have depicted similarly gruesome stories. We watch a lot of the History Channel at our house. Seeing footage of WWII, I cannot imagine seeing female bodies lying on the beaches of Normandy. I really can't. The thought is preposterous to me.

I am sure it is because my beliefs and values are still so similar to those in the 1930s and '40s. The men fighting in World War I and World War II would not have stood for their wives and daughters joining them on the front lines. They themselves joined the Armed Forces to protect their wives and children, their homes, the country they lived in, and all it stood for. They would have been crushed if they didn't have those comforting things to return home to. If women died fighting beside them, it would have seemed for naught.

What happened to this philosophy? Why can't we all hold on to some of the few precious things our forefathers fought to give us? Why are Obama, his administration, and his followers insistent on helping to tear apart all that used to make our country so powerful, united, and amazing?

CHAPTER NINE

What Women Want (from the Economy)

T HERE'S BEEN A lot of talk of late about the "gender wage gap." You know the story: women earn only seventy-seven cents for every dollar a man earns, and this is sexist and patriarchal, and Hitler totally would have loved it, and therefore the Progressives (genius saints that they are) will take it in hand and use it as a campaign platform for every candidate from now until the 2016 presidential election. President Obama brought it up in his State of the Union (SOTU) address at the beginning of 2014, presumably because he doesn't have anything else really important to talk about, prompting someone who really knows what being marginalized as a woman in the workforce means to sound the alarm.

Yes, Hillary Clinton, women everywhere relate to how tough it's been for you to rise to the top of your field as a woman. That could be related to your choice of husband but, sure, it's probably also because you're a woman and the man won't ever just let you shine like the precious diamond you are.

The problem with all the hand-wringing is that the gender wage gap has—even by esteemed mouthpieces of Progressive politics like The Daily Beast—largely been proved a myth. That publication, shortly after the SOTU, minced no words:

> What is wrong and embarrassing is the President of the United States reciting a massively discredited factoid. The 23-cent gender pay gap is simply the difference between the average earnings of all men and women working full-time. It does not account for differences in occupations, positions, education, job tenure, or hours worked per week. When all these relevant factors are taken into consideration, the wage gap narrows to about five cents. And no one knows if the five cents is a result of discrimination or some other subtle, hard-to-measure difference between male and female workers.[21]

So there it is, in no uncertain terms. Women may earn slightly less on average, but the reasons for that have to do with their choices and priorities rather than some insidious, behind-closed-doors conspiracy to keep us all barefoot and pregnant and beholden to the rightful breadwinners. This is something Conservative men and women accept as reasonable and—although Progressives have the hardest time with it—pretty cool, really. Women on the Right tend to be more comfortable with traditional gender roles and it doesn't make us feel less than capable or less smart if our husbands or men in general still serve as the hunter part of the hunter-gatherer equation. The part that Progressives—particularly the women—can't bear is that we can feel that way and also (sit down if you need to) be aggressive and ambitious, take charge of our lives (both domestically and financially), and have independent thoughts and strong convictions about our life and career goals that run *parallel* and are *equal in intensity* to those of our male counterparts. It really comes down to what we choose to focus our energy toward. And that's at the heart of the myth regarding the gender wage gap.

In the South, where I'm from, try to tell a woman she can't go out and work if she wants to. Then, seriously, duck. Because she may slap the back of your head as she jets out the door to get a job, better than yours and making more money, *just to spite you.* The point is that ever since the Equal Pay Act of 1963, it's been illegal to pay women less just because they are women. You can pay them less for other things—less education, less experience, fewer skills—but not because they wear dresses, have breasts, and tend to smell like flowers. If you do, you risk a lawsuit. And it stands to reason that if the gender wage gap is such a pressing concern that the president must address it (because he has nothing else to talk about), and all the Progressive and very underpaid women like Nancy Pelosi must stand up for their equally oppressed sisters like Facebook's Chief Operating Officer Sheryl Sandberg, there would have been a veritable avalanche of lawsuits and massive anti-discrimination payouts for the last fifty years or so. Right?

But there really hasn't been. And my guess is that's because women who recognize they make less money also recognize the reasons that may be happening. Some of us take time off to have families. Some prefer to work fewer hours. Up until recently, there haven't been any women on the show *The Deadliest Catch*, which is all about the most dangerous job in the world, commercial fishing, which also comes with a pretty hefty salary given the whole "statistically your job will kill you faster than any other job out there" thing. Personally, I consider it a mark of great intelligence that women tend to be a little more willing to balance out their personal and family life with their career aspirations, often accepting that this means they are not equal to their male counterparts (they are smarter) and must accept the consequences of those decisions. Sometimes that means less pay. But it would very likely mean the same for a man who made the decision to leave the work force for a few years to concentrate on family care, or chose to take jobs that require less education (or a different kind of education). Leave it to the Progressives to create a scandal where none exists to make sure the population is enraged enough to ignore the veritable disasters their policies have created.

And while we're on that subject, those very policies—the ones that carry the mantra of victimhood—are precisely what has led to the real problems regarding women in the workforce. Since the 1960s, women in minority communities have been told that they really don't need a man because Big Poppa Government can provide for them. Many of these women grew up knowing that having a child out of wedlock—one of the biggest predictors of financial health—would garner them a check of some kind. And the more kids, the bigger the check. Many of these women ditched school to have the kids and live a life of frustrated intellect that never realized its potential. Never mind that the check is paltry compared to what they could have been earning if they weren't duped into seeing themselves as victims who needed assistance.

What message does this send to the men of these same communities? Paul Ryan addressed it recently and got tagged a racist, while President Obama is lauded for addressing the same concerns, and without the same diplomacy of language. But Senator Ryan was talking about something human. Part of what this Progressive message of "the economy exists for you and you don't need to give back to it" does to the men in our society is that it strips them of their self-worth and forces them to find other avenues to feel like men. And the cycle continues.

The men in some of these communities recognize they have been marginalized—their worth as providers in competition with Big Poppa Government—and they behave as any man would. They do their own thing and try to find their masculinity somewhere, thwarted though it is. That's another great truth Progressive women miss about men that Conservative women tend to innately understand: men, by their very nature, *like* to be providers and are naturally inclined to protect the fairer sex. It's one of those pesky, genetically encoded things that Progressives still haven't figured out how to get right.

Big Government welfare policies have been terrible for communities in this country by making women less desiring of reaching their potential financially—either on their own merit or by marrying a man who can provide for them and their children—and it's made men not care to compete with Big Poppa Government. We have emasculated a significant portion of the male population in this country. And we've ensured that women see it as a better option not to contribute to the overall economic health of the country because it's not going to feed their families as quickly as that check that comes every month. And women are practical. They know the value of the bird in the hand.

But this isn't the gender wage gap the Progressives want to concentrate on. No, no. They prefer to attack adjectives. Because that, honestly, falls more in line with how logical most of their ideas are. One of the latest is the "Ban Bossy" campaign, helmed by that same marginalized and financially suffering Facebook COO Sheryl Sandberg. Because the word "bossy" is really the problem. I mean, sure. That makes total sense.

Kidding aside, I don't know about y'all, but I have a hard time believing the way to empower women to step up and become better providers and contributors to the general economy is to ban a word that only some women have ever been called. The "Ban Bossy" campaign is an attempt to reclaim an ostensibly negative word that, according to Sandberg, actually describes a quality that women achievers tend to have, and the quality that may be responsible for propelling them to the top. Where I come from we had another b-word for the attitude Sandberg describes and honestly, what's got me confused about this whole thing is that there's absolutely nothing wrong with being called bossy if you are, in fact, bossy. In other words, the issue isn't the word, it's the behavior. There are simply better ways to motivate people than being defined by a word, no matter what it is. And that's where I think Conservative women differ greatly from Liberal women. We all want to get ahead financially if we can—although, as mentioned, there may be radically different reasons fueling those ambitions. Conservative women tend to want a healthy economy to provide for themselves and their families while Liberal women tend to want to go on extravagant vacations they like to call "eco-tourism." The difference is how we approach those goals.

Sandberg—who made the billionaire list in early 2014, and continues to go on and off the list depending on the strength of her investments—can certainly be looked to as a woman who has useful information to offer other women regarding how to get ahead. The only problem is, she offers really bad advice that, as most studies and information indicate, doesn't actually lead to female economic happiness. And happiness is what leads to empowerment because, as my father always said: "Happy wife, happy life." Happiness itself is empowering and has the strange effect of propelling people to want more of it.

So what does Mrs. Lean-In (That's part of the title of her very popular book) have to say that is so soul-crushingly wrong for the American woman? Well, if I had to sum it up, in a highly intellectual and Wall Street way (which, of course, is definitely going to appeal to that subset of the American woman who has actually been marginalized by being encouraged to drop out of high school to have children and receive a government check), she perpetuates the myth that the Left has been shoveling like manure to women since the '60s: that we ladies are victims of the man—and not the metaphorical, fight-the-power man, but the *real* man. The patriarchy, the dudes next to us, our brothers and fathers and sons and husbands . . . they lie on us like a burka. You know them—always trying to keep us down. Right, Sheryl? I know you know, girl.

By doing this, she's funneling something that I consider pretty close to evil: she's setting up a fabricated war between the sexes that is actually one of the driving factors in why so many women are impoverished and uneducated and reliant on Big Poppa Government for their check to buy groceries and keep the bills paid. She's perpetuating the myth that men, not poor social programs, put women behind the eight ball; that men will never stick around, so you need government to give you your stuff; that men don't care about you or your children, but the benevolent federal government does. And here's the real problem with this line: the men are listening, too, and finding themselves (see above) dismissed and just as frustrated with the state of affairs as their female counterparts.

What it does to women is equally insidious. Recently at a Heritage Foundation panel celebrating Women's History Month, Conservative columnist Mona Charen had some great things to say about the myths of feminism (not, of course, to be confused with the feminist mystique, because those ideas are part of the reason some of these things have spiraled the way they have). She made a statement, referring to Mrs. Lean-In herself, who had noted that a truly equal world would see half the countries led by women, half the businesses with female CEOs, and so on and so forth. But Mrs. Charen, herself an accomplished columnist, speechwriter, thinker, and politico (as well as wife and mother to three sons) dismantled that idea pretty effectively when she pointed out that the female leader of Argentina was an abysmal failure, while Margaret Thatcher was the very successful and very respected Iron Lady. And, furthermore, Charen said, she didn't really see how either one of their stories had much to do with their gender. You see, Mrs. Charen doesn't buy the feminism myth and prefers to believe (probably because it's true . . . Conservative women having a weird affinity for the truth) that the so-called gender pay gap is a drummed-up crisis. The discrepancy in pay between men and women is more a reflection of women's choices (because we do actually have them, despite what the topless feminist at any abortion debate will tell you) and our priorities, which, it turns out, tend to be very different from our beloved men's.

THE DISCREPANCY IN pay between men and women is more a reflection of women's choices (because we do actually have them, despite what the topless feminist at any abortion debate will tell you) and our priorities.

"The Obama administration has been particularly uneducable on this subject and has subtracted from the sum total of human knowledge," Charen noted at the panel. Major points for hilarity on that one. Furthermore, she noted that family disruption—kids out of wedlock, dropping out of school, not needing to make relationships with fathers work because that check will be here soon—is what's really perpetuating income inequality. And this is an important thing to be aware of because they're going to try to tell women what we want from the economy in the next few years. They're going to be shoving it down our throats. And so women, especially Conservative women, are going to have to be on their toes to make sure we know what it is we really want from our careers, and what we really see as the mark of financial health and fiscal responsibility. And here's what those things are.

In a 2011 study titled "Unlocking the Full Potential of Women in the US Economy," the *Wall Street Journal* acknowledged that there were certainly factors that held women back and some of those factors included women being left out of peer networking channels (the boys club, if you will) and embedded organizational structures ("Everyone knows that a woman wouldn't be right for that position."). But interestingly, they also mentioned a few factors that are related mostly to the choices these women are making themselves. For example, under a subsection called, "Embedded Individual Mindsets," it noted:

> The effect of women's own mindsets cannot be discounted. While women remain highly confident of their qualifications throughout their careers, women are, on average, less satisfied than men with their chosen professions and jobs. Moreover, as women get older, their desire to move to the next level dissipates faster than men's desire. At all ages, more men want to take on more responsibility in their organizations and have greater control over results.

In other words, women themselves tend to lose the passion for advancement as they progress through their careers, while men—again, probably related to not just societal but also that pesky genetic provider tendency—keep pushing on. Intuitively, it's reasonable to guess that this may have to do with children and family. Many women from the same study expressed a dissatisfaction with the 24/7, "always on" nature of the executive.

At the same time, these women never lose their confidence in their own abilities. They just shift priorities because of another truth we Southern women are taught from birth: we have the right to change our minds. Does that sound less than empowered? Stopping midstream, changing careers, taking a break, having children *and* a career all sound like opportunities to me. So the notion that women are somehow being marginalized and discriminated against when so many opportunities exist for them seems a bridge too far.

Speaking of opportunity, the same study is pretty clear that things are way better now than they've been in the past:

> Women have been a growing factor in the success of the U.S. economy since the 1970s. Indeed, the additional productive power of women entering the workforce from 1970 until today accounts for about a quarter of current GDP. Still, the full potential of women in the workforce has yet to be tapped. As the U.S. struggles to sustain historic GDP growth rates, it is critically important to bring more women into the workforce and fully deploy high-skill women to drive productivity improvement.

So why all the outrage about how women are paid less and can't advance and there's a War on Women and a gender pay gap and *we're all just victims*? Because outrage bears fruit and those fruits are the votes of the misinformed who need to believe there's some other factor that contributes to their inability to get ahead despite dropping out of high school and never working more than a menial job. It's the Conservatives and their War on Women. Because it makes perfect sense that if only we could even up that pay gap, all women would suddenly be employed and happy. It's a ridiculous notion.

And let's talk about that War on Women for a minute. It was mildly hilarious—would have been hysterical if it weren't so sad—when it was discovered in the midst of the gender pay gap parade that the White House itself was actually paying women less than their male counterparts. Except that little factoid turned out to also be not quite true when the *Washington Examiner* reported that, at the highest levels in the White House, women were out-earning their male counterparts. Good Lord, it's like herding cats trying to pin down the half-truths and outright lies of the War on Women. Screeching, hissing cats that are convinced the men are out to get them ani pull their tails, all the while having lunchtime martinis in the secret male cloakroom. Or something to that effect.

USA Today pretty much sealed the deal on why all the screeching fails to elicit a ton of sympathy, mostly from the Right and, increasingly, from the Left:

> The problem is that comparing what all men and all women earn is deceptive. Men tend to choose more jobs that require long hours, or that are dangerous— hence the much higher rate of vocational death

among men than women—but that also pay more. Women tend to prefer jobs that offer flexible or shorter hours, and clean indoor conditions.

Indeed, as Amy Otto notes, a recent puff piece on Jay Carney in *The Washingtonian*, though largely mocked for its photoshop errors, inadvertently revealed the gender-gap cause: Carney's wife, high-profile journalist Claire Shipman, "works part-time now for *ABC News*, something she's done for five years, which has given her more flexibility to write and hang out with her children. Flexibility, she says, is what most working mothers really want."

That's probably right, but part-time jobs that give you flexibility to hang out with your kids generally don't pay as much as hard-charging jobs that keep you at the office all night. And would it be fair to the office all-nighters if they did?[22]

No, in fact, it would not. Which brings us again to the idea that if men were making the same choices as women, that gender pay gap might dissipate quicker than a morning mist in a Southern summer.

Interestingly, for all the talk about women and the economy, and addressing the "problem" of the War on Women to make sure that women are getting the same amount financially as their male counterparts, there seems to be an appalling lack of discussion about what women—real women—think of all this nonsense when all the facts are presented to them. I'd like to know, for example, if the woman who's holding down a part-time job so she can watch the kids while her husband works full-time would be willing to change that situation if she was promised she would be making that extra twenty-three cents on the dollar. Or would the young career girl busting her hump on Wall Street—who also happens to be looking for the right man because she'd like to have kids one day—be willing to sacrifice her family aspirations if the gender pay gap were, once and for all, addressed and obliterated? Or would any woman be willing to go out on one of those fishing boats in the North Sea to catch lobsters or whatever it is they do out there? I mean, no disrespect to any lady who might want to do that . . . I'm sure there may be some who exist, but it sure isn't me. The fact that there may be some who exist proves the point: who could stop them if they wanted to?

And this is where Conservative women and Liberal women part ways in dramatic fashion. Conservative women understand that the deck is not actually stacked against them in the workplace. In fact, with all the eggshells everyone's walking on these days concerning these issues, the deck is stacked decidedly in their favor. Conservative women also know that focusing on the barrier is foolish and impractical so we tend to focus on ways to get around any barrier that may exist. Sure, sexism exists in the workplace, but so do a lot of other things that affect both men and women.

I've known men who couldn't get promoted because the jerk in the corner office just didn't like the cut of their jib. But the ones who wanted it badly enough found a way to get what they sought, either by waiting out the jerk, winning over the jerk, or taking another position. These are the same options available to women. And frankly, as any woman knows, men are pretty easy to persuade if you're wickedly smart and not afraid to actually be a woman. (Think Joan Harris on *Mad Men*. The woman can command a room just by walking into it and never trying to not be the buxom beauty that she is.) Add to that a fierce intellect and a head for business and women, as my father is fond of saying, "could rule the world if they wanted to."

I'm of the opinion that the smart ones already do. And one of the ways they do it is by trying their level best not to complain that someone doesn't like them and thinks they're "bossy." Bosses are bossy. That's how it works.

Money doesn't buy happiness necessarily but it can buy a day at the spa, which makes most women very happy. Truth is, we don't have to have a large bank account and investment portfolio; however, women love stability and if we have enough to keep our lifestyle at the very least status quo, then we are happy.

I went back to work when the economic crisis of 2008 hit. I married into a family-owned building business, and the collapse of the housing market meant doom for many within the industry. Our company, like so many others, downsized to the bare minimum and most of the remaining employees, including my husband, reduced their own pay just to keep the company afloat. With our own insurance premium being almost one thousand dollars per month for a family of four, our small savings were quickly drained.

While I loved my job, I always said I wanted nothing more than to be able to stay at home with my children while they were young. But on a very limited income, there was no way we could keep our home in our community and not fall deeper in debt than we were sure we could eventually get out of.

Going back to work at the very beginning definitely did not make me happy, especially trying to keep the smile on my face and the public display of exhaustion at a minimum at the same time. Even five years later, the guilt I feel on a daily basis can be overwhelming. I refuse to let my family drop me off at the airport as I fly away to cover a story; I can't take the look on my children's faces as the car pulls away. I can assure you, at those moments, happiness is not the motivation for the tears falling down my face.

However, I am quickly reminded of the happiness my children feel every day when they walk into the safe, positive environment of our neighborhood elementary school, or the happiness I feel when I have a few extra dollars to splurge on taking them to their favorite restaurant, or to the doctor when they are sick. Finally, the happiness I get from knowing that, hopefully, if my husband and I stay as close as possible on our planned path, we will not be a financial burden on our children. This is the happiness we as responsible Conservative women seek.

So what do we want? I can only speak for the Right side of the political spectrum but the answer is pretty simple. We want to be able to eat. We want to be able to feed our families. We want to be able to take a nice vacation with our men without worrying that it'll break the bank. We want financial security. We want respect. We want our effort to be rewarded and we want a free market that continuously creates jobs where we have the flexibility to choose without being afraid we won't be able to have the things listed above.

The policies those Progressive Liberal ladies back—the policies of victimhood, the ones that insisted that our healthcare system was broken and needed fixing, the ones that have topless women harassing men at pro-life rallies in some twisted parody of empowerment—do not facilitate a free market where our choices grow. Rather, they keep many women chained to government assistance and they bankrupt an insurance system that was working pretty well when we went to the hospital to have mammograms or our babies delivered.

My guess is that Liberal women want the same things— although sometimes I really do wonder about that. But they seem to be of the opinion that they get those things by whining about inequity instead of just finding the formula that works for them and making it work. And for all the blather about sisterhood, they sure do have a healthy measure of hate when it comes to Conservative women who exercise the choice of staying at home rather than working. Columnist John Hawkins pointed this out in Townhall when he said:

> Liberals insult, demean and degrade stay-at-home moms on a regular basis. How dare they treat women with contempt simply because they CHOOSE to stay home and take care of their children? For example, Democrat Congresswoman Kyrsten Sinema has said, "These women who act like staying at home, leeching off their husbands or boyfriends, and just cashing the checks is some sort of feminism because they're choosing to live that life. That's bull . . . . I mean, what . . . are we really talking about here?" Recently, Liberal blogger Amy Glass at Thought Catalog wrote a whole article mocking stay-at-home moms called, "I look down on young women with husbands and kids and I'm not sorry." Even in the last election, when Democrats were pushing the "war on women" meme, Democrat strategist Hillary Rosen slammed Ann Romney for being a stay-at-home mom while Barack Obama himself has said staying at home to raise children isn't real "work." Conservatives support women, whether they want to work or stay at home. Liberals don't—and their utter contempt for stay-at-home moms is just as disgusting as it is revealing.

So, let's get this straight: women must go to work and fight to earn that extra twenty-three cents because that's the only true measure of a worthwhile woman. If a woman exercises any other choice—something our forebears fought tooth and nail to allow us to have—we are leeches and we're certainly not working.

Kyrsten Sinema has it wrong. How on earth does she think some families manage to be fiscally responsible? Day care is expensive so staying home is actually, in some cases, the most responsible choice when it comes to the bank book. And ya know what? Even if it wasn't, so what? We are endowed by our creator with the rights to life, liberty, and the pursuit of happiness. If that happiness means staying home while your husband brings home the bacon, then that's what it means. Fight the power!

Following the 2012 election, a contributor to *Forbes*—a woman named Carrie Lukas—had a few tips for Conservatives as they tried to get a handle on why so many women voted for Barack Obama, possibly pushing him over the edge to win. She had some interesting insights into how conservatives should frame future debates about the economy to appeal to women:

> Women need an education about how their decisions about what to study impact their future earnings, what careers and specialties to pursue to maximize earnings, and how many hours spent at their jobs will drive their long-term earning potential. They also need more information about how the

Left's "solutions" to the perceived wage gap problem—that's more government oversight over how employers compensate workers, and more lawsuits, as proposed under the Paycheck Fairness Act—can backfire in terms of reducing the availability of jobs and making the workforce less flexible.

Women need to hear how well women are doing compared to men in academia, and how the United States' historically dynamic market economy has actually been a source of great progress for women. The recent decades of technological progress, for example, has been a boon to women in terms of creating greater communication options and new paradigms for balancing work and family responsibilities.

In other words, according to Ms. Lukas, Conservatives need to get out there and start telling women the truth. Of course, the problem they face is that the truth may hurt. No one likes the idea of getting comfortable with a system of outrage only to then be told that they really have nothing to complain about and they should better themselves for the sake of themselves and their families. But that is, indeed, the economic message that needs to be communicated. And there are so many examples out there to point to who have nothing to do with perpetual anger at being marginalized.

Perhaps successful women should step up to the plate every time a Nancy Pelosi or Hillary Clinton tries to widen the divide, stop them short, and say, "No, no, no. You *can* make the economy work for you. But you must start *believing* that you can." We Conservative women know this in our hearts and our minds.

Truth is, we Conservatives just need to make sure we do just as good a job showcasing our success stories as the Left does. We must passionately convey the message that we as Conservative women don't have to justify our political party because of our gender; rather, our gender justifies our political party.

That's real empowerment.

CHAPTER TEN

Hugging Trees and Getting All Sappy

I N 2013, NEWS that former Vice President Al Gore was set to sell his small cable outfit Current TV to Al Jazeera television opened up a can of worms that the one-time Godfather of Climate Change probably would have preferred remain sealed. For one thing, the man who had won an Oscar for his documentary-style film *An Inconvenient Truth* (and it was only in the style of a documentary, because it had a somewhat tenuous relationship to the truth) was selling out to a station that not only had the reputation of being the voice of jihad but was also funded by the oil-rich nation of Qatar. So the man who would have been president except for those pesky hanging chads literally struck a deal with a nation of terrorism supporters engaged in the filthy production of oil. Inconvenient truths, indeed.

But then, anyone surprised by this news clearly needed to get out more because Gore's hypocrisy had already been widely reported a few years before. A study conducted by the Tennessee Center for Policy Research right after he won that aforementioned Oscar detailed just how much Mr. Climate Change paid to heat, cool, and keep the lights on at his estate just outside of Nashville. And at $30,000 a year, in all probability more than some folks on the margins of poverty make while trying to feed a family, the number struck some as rather . . . inconvenient.

From an *ABC News* report from 2007:

> "If this were any other person with $30,000-a-year in utility bills, I wouldn't care," says the Center's 27-year-old president, Drew Johnson. "But he tells other people how to live and he's not following his own rules."
>
> Scoffed a former Gore adviser in response: "I think what you're seeing here is the last gasp of the global warming skeptics. They've completely lost the debate on the issue so now they're just attacking their most effective opponent."

Unfortunately, this is just another example of the Left's "do as I say, not as I do" policy. They can justify why you need to be punished for not turning off your bathroom light while they keep the megawatt spotlight on their own home. They can take away your inexpensive brighter light bulb, but have no problem raising your taxes to mandate community recycling.

But isn't that just the way of Progressives, always telling everyone else what's good for them? You need a new health insurance system. Don't want it? We know what's best and you'll thank us later. You must try this new educational program Common Core. Confusing and, in some instances—especially on the math side of things—nearly impossible to figure out? Trust us . . . your kids will be better off for their frustration. Carbon caps and carbon footprint reduction policies are on the way. Expensive and tied to unreliable and questionable science, you say? But the earth is warming and the whole of humanity will be better off if you just buy an overpriced hybrid car. We know what you really want and what you really need. Meanwhile, we'll be here retrofitting our palatial estates with prohibitively expensive and useless solar panels because we care about the environment too.

Global Warming, Meet Climate Change

Anyone who's been paying attention since the '70s recognizes that the environmental movement, with its changing names and focus, has reached levels of paranoia and ecstasy that are only usually seen within the confines of religious movements and, more specifically, cults. Not only has the myth of global warming been put off by the fact that things have seemed a little colder on average over the past several winters (so much so that they had to change the scary name to "climate change" to accommodate the non-warming), but we also found out that a lot of the data supporting global warming was just a big fat lie. There was a time when you couldn't even say that publicly lest you get the stink eye from every twenty-something know-it-all who had been steeped in the Liberal cultural bias that pervades academia. However, as inconvenient as all this is, it remains the truth. Sorry, Al Gore.

Michael Mann, a climate scientist at Penn State University and the father of that infamous "hockey stick" climate graph, was so peeved that his lies were pointed out that he decided to sue the brilliant columnist Mark Steyn, the *National Review*, and the Competitive Enterprise Institute for libel because they referenced his foray away from the truth in the same breath as another famous Penn State employee—Jerry Sandusky. It was meant as a joke of course, but Mann didn't think it was funny. In the *American Spectator,* Conrad Black wrote:

> . . . this so-called "hockey stick" graph . . . was a simple image that caught on, but the reliability of the data on which it is based has been called into question by many in the scientific community, including proponents of anthropogenic climate change such as Hans von Storch of the University of Hamburg, who has called the stick model quatsch, or "nonsense."
>
> In the fifteen years since Mann stepped onto the rink with his stick in hand, data suggests that

there has been no change in world temperature . . .
Unsurprisingly a great deal of scorn has been
heaped upon the whole global warming fraternity
(and I for one have not entirely succeeded in resisting the temptation to join in the fun). But these
jabs are generally endured as fair comment, especially in the United States. Mann's lawsuit, then, is
(to continue the sports analogy) something of a last
stand by a group of struggling players at the crease
in front of their goalie.[23]

There was also the little matter of some e-mails shared between climate scientists overseas that were obvious attempts
to control the damage by covering up some of the data they
themselves found that disproved the narrative that the earth
was warming, that we were to blame, and that we needed to
funnel a ton of money into the Church of Global Warming.
The best part about all of this is that Mann is apparently not
keen on releasing his own data—you know, the data he's willing to sue over because he says it's right and it is libelous to
suggest otherwise. In fairness, he's angrier at the Sandusky
thing because he's apparently also humorless. But it's just an
illustration of the lengths the cult leaders will go to to convince people that carbon is bad and that we are a scourge
upon the earth; if we keep believing their lies they can keep
getting their questionable studies funded to the tune of lots
of money.

Never mind of course that with these lies comes the inevitable destruction of whole segments of the economy that hard-working people rely on to feed their families. I guarantee, not a single politician has won his office without mentioning the rising cost of bread, eggs, and milk. Yet, when it comes time to vote, it seems they forget the moms and dads they appealed to on the campaign trail in exchange for the environmentalist and Beltway lobbyist.

Take, for example, the recent very long and ridiculous thought piece penned by MSNBC host Chris Hayes that appeared in *The Nation*, wherein he suggests that our reliance on fossil fuels is not unlike our past reliance on slavery.

Let that sink in.

Basically, Hayes is demonizing fossil fuels and calling for their eradication because we are doing damage to ourselves as humanity by perpetrating such cruelty on the world. But in a piece at *National Review*, Tim Cavanaugh essentially explains to Hayes that fossil fuels are the reason humanity has endured at all:

> It took 2 million years or so of human history for the population of Planet Earth to reach 1 billion, early in the 19th century. A few years prior to that landmark, the continuous-rotation steam engine was invented. And by the strangest coincidence, that population number went on to increase seven-fold in only 200 years.

A perceptive person might conclude that internal combustion and the use of fossil fuels had something to do with that progress, at least by providing a range of options beyond freezing, starving, dying in infancy, or any of the other indignities that constitute most of human experience in a state of nature. A person in an expansive mood might even say exploitation of fossil fuels is a miracle.[24]

And on a more personal note, there are whole communities in West Virginia, Eastern Kentucky, and Pennsylvania that mine coal and will be out of work if we succeed in making fossil fuels evil. There are entire industries like natural gas that would fold if we decided that fracking was like selling people in the market on Sunday. There are untapped economic possibilities for so many people searching for work in this decimated economy that wait anxiously for the Keystone XL Pipeline to finally be allowed to open and start providing this country with oil so we can stop dealing with the hotbed of unrest that is the Middle East. Hayes and Mann, of course, and pretty much all the Progressives who tell us that good honest hard work of the sort that comes with efforts to heat and cool and power are tools of the devil, never have to consider what it feels like to watch a faceless bureaucratic machine dismantle your ability to earn a living. It pays well to be a shill. And so they sit in their ivory towers, and drive their cars, and take their private jets, and judge the rest of us for providing them the means to do any of those things . . . even while disturbing little reports continue to filter out debunking all their theories.

A report from the British paper *The Telegraph* in 2013 detailed such a study. In the article, the UN Intergovernmental Panel on Climate Change (IPCC) put out a statement saying the world was headed for a period of cooling. The funny part is the IPCC statement completely contradicted the computer forecasts of imminent catastrophic warming which have been touted by the global warming crazies. So at this point with two separate groups stating two separate forecasts, it becomes a personal choice as to which one you wish to believe since neither can be considered 100 percent proven and factual. All of this makes us no closer today to realizing what is going on than we were when man was first discovering fire with two sticks.

The IPCC later went on to say, "Despite the original forecasts, major climate research centres now accept that there has been a 'pause' in global warming since 1997. The original predictions led to billions being invested in green measures to combat the effects of climate change."[25]

A pause in global warming since 1997, you say? Funny, I don't remember hearing much about that when I was being told that any time a new storm made its way up the East Coast, it was because of a warming planet and man-made effects on the general climate. And notice that word "billions." That's a whole lot of money these guys stand to not get if anyone discovers that they've been continuing to rant and rave and blame and shame everyone for their behavior and how bad it is for the environment.

Changes in Industry

Now, some would argue that there are new industries that have popped up as a result of all the global warming scaremongering—like the hybrid car industry and biofuels. Except that no one wants hybrid cars because they're inefficient and expensive, and biofuels aren't even worth mentioning really because no one's really been able to get them to work, despite the Obama administration hiring a guy who was supposed to do just that, Energy Secretary Steven Chu. That biofuel craze lasted about a second because Chu really couldn't make the idea work on a grand enough scale to matter. But he is on record saying that the only way to make people amenable to his bad idea was to artificially inflate the price of gasoline so they wouldn't have much of a choice but to try his bad idea.

Truth is, the term "biofuels" sounds very academic and most Americans don't really know what they are; however, what we can all relate to is the cost of corn products. In fact, there are very few items in your grocery store today that do not have corn in their ingredient list, including unexpected products like French fries (because of vegetable oil), yogurt (high fructose corn syrup), peanut butter, and so forth. The prices of these products rise with the cost of biofuels as corn products are directly related. Therefore, it's easy to say that while biofuels might not work to make your car more efficient, they are already having a direct impact on your pocketbook.

Again, that's the whole Progressive methodology. Take something that works, demonize it, throw money at its competition, lie that the competition is better, then destroy the original working thing so that there's no choice but to use the inferior product. Sounds a lot like what's been happening in the health industry with Obamacare, doesn't it?

And let's talk about the price of gasoline going up and what kind of effect that has on both the working women as well as the moms who drive their minivans and SUVs to play-dates and soccer practices around this country. Or do we even need to? It's not rocket science that higher gas prices are just an added expense in a working family's ledger.

The latest push by the Progressives comes to us via the food or fuel debate and they hope do this because most people remain shockingly unaware of what is going on behind the scenes to make their grocery prices continue to rise. Once again, there's this story being told that we are helping the environment by reducing our reliance on crude oil and incorporating more organic and cleaner-burning materials into our gasoline.

The sad part is, these environmentalists care more about their fields of grain than the farmers who grow and harvest it. What are these environmental do-gooders doing to the agriculture industry that simply cannot meet the demand it would take to make this formula work? What about all those farmers who are calling Capitol Hill, telling their elected officials that this is an impossible task and they face a bleak future if they're forced to succeed at something that they cannot do?

I don't know about y'all, but to me there seems to be a fundamental flaw in the whole leading-from-behind, growing-from-the-middle-out, trickle-up economic theories of the current administration. And it's really just this simple: if you pressure and tax the producers in this country—in this case the coal miners, and the automobile manufacturers, and the farmers—to meet some pie-in-the-sky ideal, eventually you will break those people and those industries—the only ones that are producing—under the burdens of mandates and regulations. And then who is left to produce?

This is a basic tenet of Ayn Rand's popular-for-a-reason book, *Atlas Shrugged*. The producers in that book, however, get wise to the game and just opt out of society, forming their own mini-society away from the regulation of big government. And the workers in this country are getting wise. That's why the elections of 2010, when the Tea Party asserted itself, were so remarkable. And the way things are going, they're mobilizing again for the 2014 elections because things have gotten worse after six years of "Obamanomics."

As far as the environment goes, there was a great speech given by the late Michael Crichton some years ago where he discussed some of the fallacies of the idea that we can predict changes in the environment at all:

I have recycled my trash, installed solar panels and low flow appliances, driven diesel cars, and used cloth diapers on my child—all approved ideas at the time.

I still believe that environmental awareness is desperately important . . .

But I have also come to believe that our conventional wisdom is wrongheaded, unscientific, badly out of date, and damaging to the environment . . .

In my view, our approach to global warming exemplifies everything that is wrong with our approach to the environment. We are basing our decisions on speculation, not evidence. Proponents are pressing their views with more PR than scientific data. Indeed, we have allowed the whole issue to be politicized—red vs. blue, Republican vs. Democrat. This is in my view absurd. Data aren't political. Data are data. Politics leads you in the direction of a belief. Data, if you follow them, lead you to truth.

His speech, given at the National Press Club in Washington, DC, was called "A Case for Skepticism of Global Warming," and it's genius in its primary assertion that the environment is such a dynamic and ever-changing mess of a system that it is impossible to gather accurate data, and even if we do have data, it's impossible to use it to predict anything—either about our role in the system or how things might change in the coming years. It's just too vast a data set, much of which we don't have access to because we haven't been around long enough to accurately decide anything as far as weather systems and patterns on earth.

One of the funniest proofs of this theory came recently when I was checking the weather on weather.com and reading a story about a storm system coming up through the Gulf of Mexico. The meteorologist was quoted as saying that they simply couldn't predict the weather more than two weeks in advance—that this was an industry standard and that all weather people understood this. He had inadvertently—this weather.com weatherman—stated the simple answer to the behemoth of climate change alarmists: they can't know anything more than two weeks in advance.

In a perfect world, where America was not burdened with more than $18 trillion in debt, then we could spend taxpayer dollars on such whimsical issues; however, we do have true problems within this country which need our attention and, more importantly, our resources devoted to finding solutions.

In 2013 it was shown that the Obama administration was set to spend more on climate change stuff than it was on border security. Almost twice as much was spent fighting this unproven theory than protecting our borders from terrorists and illegals. More than $22.2 billion was spent in 2013 on a wide range of programs with the goal of fighting the global warming theory, and only $12 billion securing our border.

Therefore once again, our taxpayer dollars are being wasted on a theory, or what I am beginning to think is a Progressive magic show, while the facts of over 11.7 million illegals living in the US are being ignored.

Other (Real) Concerns

We have a real problem in this country with our borders. We have a serious problem with immigration and the burden it puts on our tax base. We have a real fear that bad people with bad intentions are getting into the country and bombing our marathons. And yet the Obama administration prefers to throw its time, money, and energy at an issue that is increasingly being debunked and has been on pause since the '90s.

That, as they say, is putting the focus in the wrong place.

So why do they do it? Why do they continue to harass us and put us out of work and keep us from finding jobs for an issue that is apparently based on faulty computer modeling data? Particularly when everyone can tell winter lasted longer this year than last?

The answer is money, friends. Just as with everything else that matters in this world, money is usually the center of the circus and the motivation of both good and evil.

Their logic is, if you care enough and are serious enough about being a good steward and good citizen of the planet, you will buy into the hype and do things to support their false economy of environmentalism. I've already mentioned solar panels and hybrid cars and biofuels, but there are also wind farms and carbon offsets to name a few more.

And about those carbon offsets that Al Gore uses as an excuse to justify living in his utility-bill monster of an estate in Tennessee—do you know what those are? Basically, "carbon offset purchases" simply mean that you agree to pay to have a tree planted or support some pre-approved environmental cause through some company to justify your need to have those high utility bills. Plant a tree, keep the lights on in the pool house all night long if you want, kid!

Recently, according to Reuters, all those environmentally conscious soccer fans can get their carbon footprint neutralized for free so they should just come on down to Brazil and stop worrying that they're hurting the world. FIFA, soccer's governing body, released a statement saying it would cover the cost to neutralize the carbon emissions related to travel.

I guess I missed that magic wand for sale at World Market because I don't understand: if they can just make the carbon emissions disappear for the World Cup, why don't we just do it for the entire world every day and then we won't have a problem and I can get my bright light bulb back?

The key world in all of this is *neutralized*. Which reminds me a lot of neutering; however, in this case nothing is removed. Rather those soccer fans are being given a sort of environmental purgatory for their carbon sins.

The way this happens is that the footprints are neutralized because the nonprofit organization sponsoring the initiative to get people to go to a dangerous city to see a dangerous game will invest in green companies that are doing things to be environmentally conscious. In this case those projects haven't yet been announced . . . but do you really need to know? No, of course you don't. All you need to know, green traveler, is that it's taken care of. You won't be damaging the world by flying in that nasty jet. FIFA's got you covered.

Sounds really silly, doesn't it? Sounds like a scam and just an overt attempt at collusion between green companies and the soccer organizations to get people to come to the game. It's a fair bet, too, that people who maybe wouldn't go might go just so they can brag about doing the world some good because they offset their carbon footprint. They did their part.

Sometimes the stupidity is exhausting.

And about those companies and projects . . . often they are owned by some of the biggest pushers of green policy like, say, Al Gore. So when Al Gore says he's buying carbon offsets to justify paying $30,000 a year in utility bills and owning several houses and jetting around in a gas-guzzling private jet, he's literally talking about taking money out of one of his pockets and putting it into the other.

And that's the way the church of environmentalism works. Back before Protestantism existed, the Catholic Church had a system that was very similar to the carbon-offset scam. It was called buying an indulgence. Basically, you were allowed to sin if you paid the church to intercede for you with God, give you a little nod in his direction, let him know you were a good egg and you didn't mean any real harm. And this is what led to Martin Luther stomping his way down to the church, nailing his ideas about this particular scam to the church doors, and creating an entire new denomination born of the need not to be taken in by a moneymaking scheme for suckers. So the question is, who is the modern-day Martin Luther standing up for the coal miners and the oil drillers and the farmers in the face of Pope Michael E. Mann and the bishops in the Obama administration?

So step back, examine the evidence, and realize that the church of environmentalism is selling you indulgences so you don't have to worry about the sins of your excess—and in the process, destroying the economy, shaming people into bad behavior, and ruining whole industries that have contributed to the health and well-being of mankind since the Industrial Age.

Many on the Left would like to paint today's Conservative as being as cold as the handshake between Vladimir Putin and President Obama at the G20 summit in 2013; however, truth be told, Conservatives are the honest environmentalists. We realize that when we encourage a more responsible, stable, prosperous environment, people are more willing to take care of their own property and preserve it as well as the environment around it for future generations.

Conservatives don't like a game of smoke and mirrors and while we can forgive, we don't forget when we have been purposely deceived as in the case of many of these conflicting environmental studies. We are informed; therefore, you cannot just win us over with an emotional image of a dying animal or plant. Rather, we see the numbers and don't believe in most cases it's worth adding more to the unemployment rosters to save a spotted owl.

Our honest love and respect for this earth we have been blessed with needs to be shown as often as possible. We need to do exactly the opposite of what the Left does, and show the depth of our motivation for taking care of the earth, but not because we have an ulterior motive. Rather, we have an ultimate motive of making sure we leave this world in better shape than when we came in. We do this in regard to everything else in our daily life. Yet because the environmental movement has been almost completely hijacked and corrupted by the Progressives, we are quick to avoid any cause remotely involved in environmental preservation.

Thankfully, God himself may have stepped in with all the unpredictable weather patterns and nailed his own set of ideas to the church door. I only hope one of the few remaining iridescent light bulbs was still hanging overhead or else we might not be so sure he could see where the actual door was.

CHAPTER ELEVEN

There is Nothing Healthy about Obamacare

W OMEN, LISTEN UP. One of the most important parts of your life is the health-care decisions you make and how you talk about them. When you look at what has happened to health care in this country, with Obamacare making health-care costs soar, decreasing your access to the plan you want and the doctors you like, and providing government subsidies for abortion, you may throw your hands up in frustration at the whole system.

Don't get me wrong . . . a health-care reform bill was in order. Health-care costs were skyrocketing with no end in sight; entitlement programs saddle the next generation with mountains of debt without providing a safety net; people who are unemployed had few options for health care; and lawsuits were putting dozens of doctor's offices out of business, if the malpractice insurance didn't do it first.

Americans deserve health-care reform that increases access to care, increases choice for providers, bends down the cost curve, and creates a safety net for those who need one without violating constitutional principles of life, liberty, and the pursuit of happiness. Obamacare doesn't deliver on those key principles; in fact, the law has made life harder for men, women, families, and businesses.

Why Health Care?

But I want to start at the very beginning. Often I am asked by women why health-care decisions are important and what they are, because this will impact your dating life, your personal life, your mental health, and how you feel on a daily basis.

Like most Americans, I want accessible, affordable, quality care with plans that respect the divisions between church and state and government and business. I want to be able to see the doctors I trust and know at a price I can afford; I want the opportunity to choose a health-care plan that works for me and my family; and I want a government that isn't going to make my life more complicated.

More than anything, I want to live in a country where I can make a good living, work my way toward success, have the freedom to provide financial security, and have a loving and healthy family.

In reality, Obamacare has directly caused at least 5.5 million Americans to lose their health insurance, despite the president's promise that you could "keep your plan if you like it." The latest numbers reported by Fox showed that the number of cancellations out-of-compliance with Obamacare had grown to 6.3 million.[26]

The problem is that people on the other end of the political spectrum don't want to examine what went wrong with health-care reform. To them, the problems are temporary and the battle has been won and reexamining the foundations of Obamacare is a pointless, partisan exercise.

Let's just take a look at some episodes over the past few years:

- Abortion? According to them, it should be available "on demand" for anyone who wants it.
- Birth control? It should be free and subsidized by taxpayers.
- Planned Parenthood? It should receive federal funding because it provides essential health-care services.

To some people, each of these arguments has been resolved and is set in stone. But it doesn't make any sense to me at all why we should talk about abortion like it's an HBO series we can watch "on demand," why private companies should be forced to give products away for free, or why for-profit abortion businesses should get a dime of taxpayer money. What if you don't want to buy health insurance under Obamacare? You'll get charged for that, $95 per adult and $47.50 per child (up to $285 for a family) or 1 percent of your taxable income, whichever is greater, and that fee will increase each year.

Reminds me of a joke Jimmy Fallon told right after the White House claimed it had hit its target: "The White House says it has surpassed its goal for people enrolled in Obamacare. It's amazing what you can achieve when you make something mandatory and fine people if they don't do it and then keep extending the deadline for months," Fallon quipped. "It's like a Cinderella story. It's just a beautiful thing. You make everyone do it."

"If you still haven't enrolled, you might have to pay a penalty called the 'Individual Shared Responsibility Payment,' which is 1 percent of your salary," he continued. "Then Americans said, 'Hey, good thing I don't have a job!'"

President Obama came into office with a laser focus on getting that health-care bill passed, ignored every idea that was outside of his Progressive viewpoint, and rammed the health-care bill through both houses of Congress using every procedural tactic on the books. Democrats refused to meet with Republicans before, during, or after the passage of the health-care bill. The President refused to acknowledge Democrats who stood against subsidies for abortion. I guess he thought people would see the train coming and get out of the way, but instead we are staying strong.

How can we forget the smug look on Speaker Pelosi's face as she marched up the steps of Congress with the gavel in her hand . . . a true PR stunt, as it reminded me of what a carnival barker would do to attract as much attention as possible. Only now can we look at that strut and realize it was more of a death march. Despite Nanny Nancy infamously saying, "We have to pass the bill so that you can find out what is in it," we still cannot guarantee that she has read more than a paragraph of the 2,074-page bill.

So I want to spell out how we are going to start getting these policies right. It begins with the conversations you have with your friends, your families, and your co-workers, because the case isn't closed.

As Michelle Malkin, a fellow Conservative woman, said, "Silence is complicity. Speak now or surrender your ground." We might have a new health-care law, but this is America. Though our health-care system is broken, it's up to us to keep our democracy intact. Some days it might feel like we live in a "demo*crazy*" but I assure you, the more we start Conservative conversations, the more people will listen.

Our Conservative principles are worth standing up for. Margaret Thatcher, one of my heroes from the other side of the pond and the first woman prime minister of England, said, "We want a society where people are free to make choices, to make mistakes, to be generous and compassionate. This is what we mean by a moral society; not a society where the state is responsible for everything, and no one is responsible for the state."

A Starting Point

So where do we begin when we want to start a conversation about what it takes to build a health-care policy that provides for choices, rewards responsible choices, and allows us to be compassionate toward those in need?

We start with stories. Women are great storytellers. Every time I get together with my girlfriends we talk about politics, our jobs, restaurants, recipes, our latest workout routines, and of course, men. Or let's just call them boys, because with a few rare exceptions, including the wonderful husbands of my dear friends, most of them are still boys.

So I want to start with a story about how I started to become aware of my body.

When I was growing up, my mom used to talk me about her high school boyfriends. She would tell me stories about wearing the letterman jacket of a cute football player, going to dances and her big-time love whom she dated from her senior year of high school through college. A lot of these stories made things I saw watching *Grease* over and over again come alive—how cool that girls still got letterman jackets in those days! I imagined my mom was Sandy and all the boys wanted her but she kept them at bay.

Alongside those stories, I would hear about the girls too, and I learned a new concept: "the dirty leg." All the greatest villains in my mom's high school stories—at least the women—were called dirty legs; they were the ones who went too far with guys in high school and there was some notion they may have had an STD, or worse.

Between the possibility of facing charges of being called a dirty leg, and just an all-out fear of sex drilled into me by her as well, my main takeaway from these conversations was that intimate interactions were probably insanely frightening.

One afternoon, I was in my mom's closet, which was one of my favorite places to be in our house. The best thing in the closet was buried behind all of the clothes—it was the box that contained stacks of muted color photos taken years earlier of my mom and her friends, who looked more glamorous than Scarlett O'Hara and the girls on the pages of my *Seventeen* magazine combined.

I admired their confidence, beauty, and poise. They were the opposite of the "dirty legs" my mom talked about and in my eyes, my mom and her friends looked like they were ready to take on the world. And they were.

All across this country there are rituals that bring women into the next phase of life—quinceañera, a sweet-sixteen birthday party, a debutante ball, a high-school prom, a sorority party, and graduation. The common thread among these ceremonies is that friends gather together to celebrate, over and over again, the momentous occasion of a woman reaching adulthood.

These are often moments when you feel most beautiful and confident, and at the same time, you are dealing with new, often unfamiliar situations, and you begin to realize that you are starting to make decisions as an adult, not a girl. I want to talk about the whole ritual of all of these events—from proms to sorority socials to moments in high school where you or your friends learn the ropes of making out and test the boundaries.

Which all leads me to say, what does it mean to be a responsible, Conservative woman in today's world?

Becoming Responsible

Every mother wants her daughters and granddaughters to enter the world with the principles, information, and knowledge they need to protect themselves and build prosperous lives.

Now that there is more information available than ever, it's more essential than ever that we equip ourselves, our friends, and our daughters with the principles that will help them make responsible decisions to seize opportunities and make decisions about sex that benefit themselves, and ultimately make their communities stronger.

When you are alone outside of the protective wings of your parents, what sticks with you are your principals and your memories. If you have strong, positive, Conservative values and mentors, they will get you away from a bad situation quickly. If you don't have them, you could get way off track.

This always reminds me to be the best-possible mentor I can, and understand that in a very real way, the choices I make influence others. We may not realize it but our little cousin, sister, or friend who is in college is watching our every move to see how we interact with men, how we use our bodies, and what we wear. Believe me, she is.

We need to treat our bodies with the utmost respect. I think we need to start by getting comfortable with talking about our bodies, because when we say something out loud, when we give something a name (anything from our house-plants to our pets to our babies) we truly begin to value it.

Anyone who has been babysitting lately or who has boys of their own knows that most creatures with XY chromo-somes are perfectly comfortable with their bodies. Boys don't have the same sense of secrecy—and sometimes shame—that comes from being a woman and developing a body that goes through menstruation, the loss of virginity, pregnancy, and childbirth.

There are two people in my life who have taught me to be comfortable, respectful, and responsible for these areas of my body: my incredible gynecologist and the amazing woman who waxes my bikini line during bathing suit season. Together, they have taught me two valuable lessons: always be proactive in taking care of your health, and don't be afraid to ask questions if something unusual is going on with your body. Even getting your period can be a terrifying experience if you are not prepared.

This is where stories from women we trust and guidance from family, friends, community leaders, and church leaders come into play.

And guess what? At the intersection of how we think about women's bodies and how we talk about them is the place where this extraordinarily *private* and important issue smacks right up against something extraordinarily *public:* health-care policy in America. Our language about health care literally shapes the policies that are being made in Washington and in every state across the country, and it impacts elections.

The health-care choices available to you right now impact the decisions you can make about the health of your body.

THE HEALTH-CARE CHOICES available to you right now impact the decisions you can make about the health of your body.

Under Obamacare, there will be more insurance cards but fewer choices, reduced access to health care, and higher costs.

On the health-care exchanges, only one, two, or three insurance carriers offer insurance in each state. With the lack of competition, there are fewer choices for you to decide what kind of health insurance you want. Your plan may have been one of the millions that didn't make the cut under Obamacare.

With more insurance cards issued through the exchange, demand will spike. The combination of a shortage of doctors and nurses, and limited insurance networks, will create a bottleneck in access. Individuals on the exchanges will likely experience a narrowing of networks and limited providers.

If you are a twenty-seven-year-old buying insurance on the health-care exchange, you will find your costs will double or more than double, according to the Heritage Foundation. For families, costs are projected to rise by more than 10 percent and fifty–year–olds can expect their costs to go up 50 percent or more.[27]

The people in Washington who rammed through the health-care bill haven't even been reliable to implement the provisions, adding uncertainty to the mix while they were destabilizing an entire marketplace.

In reality, the health-care bill paved the way for a massive government takeover of the entire health-care industry and promised the moon to American voters. But the final product provided none of the structures or incentives needed to deliver on those goals.

Here's the good news: Conservatives are being elected in state legislatures, at the federal level, and as governors. But we need to keep our eye on the prize; we need to focus on the presidency because that's where the opportunity exists to make changes to our government that will reduce the overbearing role of government. Our government should support a strong and growing economy, pave the way for more people to achieve success, and not tax us into oblivion.

During the last presidential election cycle, I had lots of girlfriends who weren't really involved in politics but were starting to get excited about Rick Perry. I asked one of my friends what appealed to her about Rick Perry. She replied that he seemed like a threat to Romney, and there was pretty much zero excitement about Romney. That's what we need to change. We need candidates we are excited about that we can actually get elected into office.

If we are being honest, during the 2012 election cycle when Conservatives were poised to lead, something always kept coming up. Conservatives looked insensitive to low-income families (thanks, Mitt Romney, for writing off 47 percent of people in this country), incapable of empathizing with women who have been raped (nod here to Todd Akin), and downright judge-freakin-mental (thanks, Mike Huckabee, for saying our libidos are out of control).

When gaffes like those happen, I can get seething mad at the people who create obstacles that make Conservatives sound unreasonable—the worst part being that those people are often on our team!

When those moments happen, I try to keep calm and remember that while Conservative principles never change, every day is a new opportunity to frame the way we talk about our beliefs. Conservatives are here for the long haul and we need to live the ups and downs of learning how to talk about what we believe. Every misstep and every time we make a ton of people mad help us identify what exactly we need to be doing.

And let's face it; some of the people holding court in the public arena of Conservative thought don't have a clue about how to talk about this incredibly important issue of women's health care and women's bodies.

Birth (Control) Rights

Like most women, I have spent my life working hard to make responsible decisions that helped me build the life I wanted. I wanted to start a family and I did it when I was prepared to do so.

The typical American woman who wants two children, spends about five years total either pregnant, postpartum, or trying to become pregnant, and more than three-quarters of her reproductive life trying to avoid pregnancy. By my math, that's thirty years avoiding pregnancy! I'm exhausted just thinking about it.

I think everybody in this country can agree that babies should be brought into this world with intention, a sense of responsibility, and love. The best way to take action is to protect yourself, should you choose to have sex before you plan to have a child, and prevent pregnancy.

Birth control is part of being responsible and responsibility is a core Conservative principle. Of course, abstinence and keeping sex within a monogamous marriage relationship is the best, most responsible choice you can make. Just know, though, that if you elect to have sex without intending to get pregnant, the more you take care of yourself by using birth control, the better off we will be as a country.

Contraceptive use is common among women of all religious denominations. More than 99 percent of women aged fifteen to forty-four who have ever had sexual intercourse have used at least one contraceptive method. Okay, so that means pretty much everyone has used a condom, taken birth control, had an intrauterine device inserted—you get the idea.

Eighty-nine percent of sexually active Catholics and 90 percent of sexually active Protestants currently use a contraceptive method, and a lot of us are married.[28]

Birth control, as the name would imply, puts women in the driver's seat of their reproductive health and that is a good thing.

In 2010, 37 million women in America were sexually active. Many of these women did not wish to become pregnant and were using contraceptives. Of these, however, 19.1 million did not use birth control because they could not afford to buy birth control in some form because they were making an income 250 percent below the poverty level, or they were younger than twenty.[29]

These are two harsh realities in the US today—and when I say birth control isn't the silver bullet for women's health care, I point to these two statistics. The first overarching problem is the lack of growth and jobs and prosperity in America, leaving 51 percent of women without the ability to access critical health-care services! That's an issue that starts with building opportunity in this economy.

When we have a slow economy that's held down by rules and red tape coming from Washington, and women who operate without the health education and access to care they need, we end up with a lot of babies born into poverty. And that just isn't the America we want to leave for the next generation.

If we think that the government "owes" us birth control, then that means we are dependent on the government. Why would we want that? The more we invite the government to take care of us, the less we will take care of ourselves.

One unexpected influence that is putting more women in the driver's seat of their own reproductive health is the MTV show *16 and Pregnant*. According to the *Washington Post*, "*16 and Pregnant* didn't inspire viewers to have kids; it inspired viewers to use contraception . . . [and] led to a 5.7% reduction in teen births—a percentage that accounts for one-third of the total decline in teen births: 20,000 fewer teen births a year."[30]

Birth control is not the foolproof, perfect solution many people think it is. Increased availability does not eliminate all unintended pregnancies, and mass distribution of contraceptives correlates with a mass increase in sexual activity.

Unfortunately, those who are currently controlling the health-care conversation would have you believe that if we get the pharmaceutical companies to give out free birth control, we'll solve all of our problems.

A government study from the Centers for Disease Control shows a clear link between birth control and the increases in sexually transmitted diseases (STDs) like herpes, human papilloma virus, chlamydia, gonorrhea, and HIV.

The same correlation exists between STDs and the increased availability of Plan B, aka emergency contraception (or "morning-after" abortion pills). A 2012 study from Christine Durrance at the University of North Carolina at Chapel Hill found increased access to Plan B resulted in higher rates of STDs, specifically gonorrhea. Worse, most research around increased availability of Plan B does not show a decreased incidence of pregnancy or abortion.

As I've already said, women's health starts in conversations within families, and should focus on proactive prevention of pregnancy and health of women. Birth control is one pathway and taking it is a choice.

A Better Plan

What we need to figure out as Conservatives is how to prevent abortions—to reduce demand and pave the way toward putting for-profit abortion businesses like Planned Parenthood out of business. Women considering abortion should seek counseling from providers that will help them cope with pregnancy and hopefully consider adoption instead. As Kathleen Parker writes, "Once a pregnancy is viewed as a human life in formation, rather than a 'blob of cells,' it is less easy to terminate the contents of one's vessel."

A Gallup poll in 2012 found that 50 percent of Americans describe themselves as "pro-life," putting the number of people who are pro-responsibility, pro-liberty, pro-freedom at an all-time high, whereas the number of Americans who believe in terminating pregnancies is at an all-time low.

According to the Constitution, Plato, and the foundations of our government, a democracy should reflect the will of the people. Despite overwhelming support for life and liberty, under President Obama's health-care law, taxpayer-funded insurance plans can cover abortion. Any person who enrolls in a plan that covers abortions will have to pay the so-called "abortion surcharge," an additional monthly fee—but you may not know if your plan covers abortions and may not be able to opt out.

The world according to Liberals is a world where every woman can have as much sex as she wants and then decide how many births or abortions on demand she wants to have. Why are women getting abortions? Shame, fear of an inability to handle the cost and stress of motherhood, an absent partner, and a zillion factors really. Let's not pretend that motherhood isn't scary—it is! Every married woman who plans to get pregnant and does will tell you that it can be as terrifying as it is an absolute blessing.

By shining a light on all of the wonderful opportunities for adoption and learning about motherhood, and acknowledging that every woman's body is important, any woman in America who gets pregnant should not be ashamed.

I am saying, let's be more thoughtful. Let's be more intentional. Let's educate our girls in school about how to be proactive in taking care of their bodies. And if they fail—because we're human and we do—let's really talk about the positive, life-giving, caregiving options that exist for women who have sex and get pregnant before they are ready.

It is kind of crazy of how many women get abortions today. Half of pregnancies among American women are unintended, and four in ten of these are terminated by abortion. Abortion businesses like Planned Parenthood are a million-dollar industry. For people to pretend if the government stops funding Planned Parenthood that women won't have access to routine health-care services is crazy. If the government decides it doesn't want to give money to Planned Parenthood, that's its prerogative.

Planned Parenthood makes millions and millions of dollars off of abortions and uses that money to elect Liberals. In 2011, Planned Parenthood spent more than one million dollars electing Democrats. That's how they make money and that's what they want to do. I think it's wonderful that they do pap smears and breast exams. They have this wonderful reputation, but the reality is that they make money from abortions. If Planned Parenthood services are so wonderful, then they need to figure out how to survive as a for-profit business.

Then Democrats call the protesters in favor of Wendy Davis "Reproductive Rights Activists." Explain to me how abortion is a "reproductive right"; isn't reproduction about having a kid? I don't consider an abortion "health care"; it's more like plastic surgery . . . it's elective.

They are trying to make it as common and uncontroversial as getting your teeth cleaned. It's a life-altering decision. It's our right to kill a baby. Abortion is not health care. A Quinnipiac survey found that 72 percent of Americans opposed funding abortions through any federally run health plan—Liberals and Conservatives. The decision is between you, your doctor, and your baby.

Can you explain to me why we are even talking about whether women can have an abortion after twenty weeks? I want to focus more energy on preventing abortion. It's a complex issue that must be approached with a strong sense of principles.

The real question is not whether it's okay to abort a baby before twenty weeks, or if it's barbaric to abort a fetus that has hands, feet, and a beating heart. The question is why people, and women like Wendy Davis, are spending time drawing lines in the sand when we should be focusing our energy on *prevention* of pregnancy and *prevention* of abortion.

I would rather see Wendy Davis stand on the floor of the Texas state legislature arguing for a taxpayer-funded bill to educate women about their options for counseling and adoption, if they have gotten pregnant before they are prepared for motherhood.

There are amazing privately funded nonprofit organizations that are making a huge impact helping women who can't afford proper health care remain sexually active and get pregnant—there are safety nets for them too. Because in America we want every single baby conceived to have the opportunity to live a full life. Nonprofit pregnancy resource centers, often located across the street from Planned Parenthoods, exist to help women facing unplanned pregnancies by offering free counseling, health care, and adoption services.

Women have choices, and we believe in increasing access to those choices. Every woman should know that they have the opportunity to get the support they need when they are scared, pregnant, and unprepared.

One of my favorite charities is a group called Decisions, Choices & Options (DC&O), which was started in 2002 as the result of a crisis pregnancy. A young woman finding herself pregnant at fifteen initially chose adoption; however, after her classmates became negative about her plan, she decided to go another path.

A teacher at her school, Joi Wasill, heard about what happened to her young student and the negative stigma around the idea of adoption. Joi realized that there was a strong need for correct information in regard to adoption and the process to be available for young mothers.

It started with a simple presentation at a high school. But the feedback from students and teachers was so overwhelming that Joi knew she had found her calling.

Today, DC&O is continuing to grow and share the positive message about adoption. Speakers range from young ladies who have been put in an unplanned pregnancy situation to beauty-pageant queens who could not get pregnant and were blessed with a baby themselves through adoption.

The group has presented to over fifty high schools in Tennessee and is included in the health, wellness, and family life curriculum in schools in Alabama, Mississippi, Missouri, North Carolina, Texas, and Ohio.

Since 2002, over forty thousand teens have heard the abstinence-based presentation of Decisions, Choices & Options, and the organization continues to grow as more schools open their doors and welcome this message.

It is because of groups like DC&O that society's view of the pregnant woman has changed. No longer are young girls who are put in this situation seen as outcasts or sent off to an "aunt" until after the baby is born and she can return without revealing her secret. This was the case in the past for so many. We hear of horror stories of newborn babies ripped out of their young mother's arms despite the screaming and tears of both.

In a time when infertility is such a problem, adoption has become a miracle for so many couples. With international adoption laws becoming more complicated and expensive, domestic adoptions have become more prevalent.

Liberals want the government to pay for everything. People are in that mentality because Liberal policies enable it.

It's Our Choice

The more intentional we are as women—whether it's our next career move, whom we date, or when we choose to have children and start a family—the healthier and better off we will become. It's critical to our ability to go out and create the best possible life we can for ourselves and our future, whether that future means starting a family or not. Conservative principles are ultimately an affirmation of everything this country is about: freedom, self-determination, and faith in our God-given ability to take charge of our future.

Women need to be the ones who are out in the forefront talking about health care. We want to help other women achieve success for themselves and make responsible decisions for our own bodies, our own families, and our own future.

You need to hear positive messages about the kinds of opportunities that exist in America, especially if you grow up in a situation where everything is against you. Government needs to partner with the people in incentivizing success, not trying to fabricate success. Instead, our government incentivizes failure or mediocrity, instead of being a safety net.

We need to encourage women to be as ambitious as possible. Today, women have immense opportunities for education and achievement. Women earn 60 percent of college degrees in this country. In fact, millennial women are graduating at a higher number then men. Millennial mothers are seen to be just as ambitious as their male counterparts and, whether it's to survive or by choice, are not just opting to stay at home and raise the children.

WE NEED TO encourage women to be as ambitious as possible. Today, women have immense opportunities for education and achievement.

Despite the president saying he cares for women, his policies indicate exactly the opposite. Today, 3.7 million *more* women are living in poverty than when President Obama took office, a direct result not of Republican legislative efforts but of the so-called "compassionate Left." Because of the escalating demands put on business, the job market has become extremely restricted.

One of my favorite quotes is from health-care executive Kristen Peck, who was asked what women bring to the table in the workplace. Let's all take one second to imagine that we live in a world where the contributions of women are a given, rather than a question! But Kristen said something that has stuck with me.

> Women bring fresh thinking. They bring a willingness to listen and to learn and to reach. They bring a special ability to connect people and ideas. In my experience, women often see connections that others do not and figure out how to build a bridge when others are still measuring the chasm. The world is crying out for the kinds of approaches women are able to bring. To move the world forward, women need to work hard and get the best education they can, look for role models who share your values and interests and speak up for what you want and need.

LET'S ALL TAKE one second to imagine that we live in a world where the contributions of women are a given, rather than a question!

Sheer force of will, luck, and relationships will get you far in life. I like what Kristin says because she encourages us to make intentional decisions—about the connections we make, the education we attain, and how we use those assets to create new connections.

Every situation can be our stage to connect new people with Conservative principles. Sometimes, studies show it can take women to the age of sixty to feel like we are able to voice our opinion and feel strong. Let's start earlier. Every woman is an authority because every woman has the power to influence.

CHAPTER TWELVE

The Brutal Truth

J UST AS WITH any subject that bothers a woman, it's usually at the very end where you find the truth about why they are upset. This is the part of the book where I become completely blunt. If you think I have held my tongue on anything up until this point, I can assure you I am not holding it now.

I am a dork . . . a fat dork, to be honest with you. At least that is how I view myself. I wrote this book for many reasons but mainly to share the struggles I have lived through and what it has taken for me to get where I am today and find the courage to not be afraid to ROAR.

Life is extremely rough and for some it's even harder. I have never been one of those who was just handed an opportunity on a silver platter and, unfortunately, I was born with the need to never settle.

In high school, what girl doesn't want to be the popular head cheerleader who dates the captain of the football team and is president of the student body? I would have been happy with just one of those or anything close to it. I was like the high-school girl in one of those Taylor Swift videos except I was much more chunky and couldn't sing nearly as well.

In fact, I was that girl in high school who was in every club possible, tried out for everything and volunteered for anything, all with hopes of convincing myself that because my calendar was full, that meant people liked me. Call it only-child syndrome or just being a girl, but I am plagued with the need to be wanted.

This can be good and it can be bad. On one hand, people who have this quality are usually pretty loyal and extremely hard workers. However, this desire to be included and wanted also gives us very low self-esteem and low confidence, as it seems we can never be loved enough.

During my junior year, I ran for student-body secretary and thought this would be my chance to finally be accepted. The day the speeches were being given will always be imprinted in my mind. I had prepared a speech with what I thought to be the clever theme of using all of the titles from current TV shows. I found it to be humorous and witty, and foolproof in showing how "hip" I was. It was going smoothly up until I said, "If I don't get elected, I know *Life Goes On*" (remember that show?) and someone in the crowd yelled out that they hated the show. Being nervous already, I thought he was yelling something about me . . . and I am convinced the entire audience did too because they laughed and gasped.

It was as if my worst nightmare was coming true. Here I was, this great speech-giver (another one of my clubs), and this was supposed to be my place to shine. And now I was having to fight back tears and stumble through the rest of the speech with my face on fire and my body feeling like rubber.

Needless to say, I never had a chance of winning and after the speech debacle I was begging my mother to let me go back to homeschooling. Wise as always, my mother responded with the words I have learned to live by: "Success is the best revenge."

Know Your Enemy

Mean people have always existed in this world. I don't forecast any scientific wonder which can remove the evil gene. Which stage you are in life determines which gender dominates the role.

The number-one enemy of a woman (Conservative or Liberal) is another woman. While we as women like to sometimes use the excuse that it's the man who's holding us down or the man who's given us this glass ceiling, truth be told it's because these limits have been set mostly by those of our own gender.

Women are more competitive than men. Women are more manipulative than men. Women are more irrational than men and, most importantly, women are meaner then men.

Now, I am sure there will be some feminist who might read this and immediately bristle. Truth be told, down in your heart you know I am right. As women, we have all run across other women who have caused us pain and stress. In some cases you might be lucky enough to only have one of these situations, but more than likely I'd bet you can think of numerous examples of where you have encountered serious conflict or hostility with another woman.

It is because of these types of negative interactions that many women today become calloused and guarded professionally and sometimes personally. The old cliché goes, "It is better to have loved and lost than never to have loved at all." This isn't always true as those whom we allow closest to us are the ones who can hurt us the most.

Every once in a while I run across a woman whom I could never imagine has ever had a conflict with anyone . . . a woman so sweet, honest, gentle, and caring that I could not imagine anyone ever having a cross thought about her. However, if you ask that woman whether she thinks everybody likes her or if she has always gotten along with everyone, even *she* will say she has had conflict. We all know these women and they are the kind of women we almost feel guilty befriending because they truly give unselfishly and see us as we wish everyone could see us—unrealistically perfect.

I will be the first to admit I am guilty in this area. In fact, some of the conflicts I have been a part of with other women have caused laws to be changed in some environments and women to get therapy. I would like to blame this on growing up as an only child accustomed to being the center of my parents' attention. But since I hate excuses, the truth is, I was just wrong in how I handled most of these conflicts . . . a truth I can now admit.

Girls have always been mean to other girls. If you have never been the target of a she-devil, then please share with me your secret. The problem is, there is no right way to deal with them. As a young child, we could tattle on them and they would get in trouble. Now, as the adult, we have no one to tell and have to deal with the mean girls face-to-face.

The good news is, as we get older, in some situations we have the luxury of just going the other way. I love when this is the option; however, sometimes we have to deal with the person because they are either in our social circle or professional environment. I hate when this is the case and frankly I have learned to forgive but not forget. These relationships cannot end well and the ball of drama is just going to continue to grow. What you need to do is just find a way to distance yourself because if you stay around, no matter what you do, more than likely you will still end up looking like the bad guy.

I have a great boss; however, he has a different management style than I am used to. He doesn't like to micromanage and believes he hired you to do your job, accomplish your task, and work out any conflicts among yourselves. In fact, the only people I have ever seen him dismiss were those who could not resolve issues themselves and seemed to constantly create drama. This type of boss, while challenging, has actually made me learn the important concept of never presenting a problem without being prepared with a solution. This is extremely valuable in life and politics.

Throughout life, I have always looked for a way to define myself, to be like the others. I wanted a group I could identify myself with. In high school, I found it in the color guard but never really fit in there. I had great grades because I always did my work and turned in every assignment, but in the marching band, I was at the bottom of the curve.

Next, I went to college and thought by joining a sorority, I finally had my identity; but even then I was never a part of the "cool kids." Being the overachiever, I always had great grades and held all of the leadership positions around campus, but amongst my own sorority sisters, I was still a dork.

After graduation, I think I finally started to forgive myself for not being the person whom everybody loved to be with. While I drove my first boss and team crazy with my smiley-face rug and Christmas lights in my cubicle, they had to love me because, while my obnoxiously optimistic attitude might have been annoying in the office, I always held my water with the team.

A Turnaround on the Friend Front

Friends were different at this point. I continued my habit of joining as many civic organizations for young adults as I could, like Junior League of Nashville, Rotaract, The Nashville Junior Chamber of Commerce, and Young Republicans of Williamson County. But oddly enough I finally gathered a group of friends who, after twenty-one years of life, were not friends with me because of what I could do for them. They actually liked me for me. Seriously?

This was a first and the lessons I learned from these women about life are irreplaceable. Being the youngest in the group, I was able to watch these eleven young professional women deal with life. What I was most amazed with is all eleven had separate lives full of work and other friends, but our base was always each other. We didn't care if one person made more money than the other or if one was prettier than another; we all appreciated each other for each one's character. We celebrated each other's accomplishments and cried with each other's losses. We didn't see color or differences. This was the group of women who finally healed my wounds of the past enough for me to feel secure to start roaring a little louder.

Today, my husband, family, and close friends give me that security; however, that doesn't mean that I am not feeling like I am constantly disappointing them. These days, I feel like I say "I'm sorry" more then I say anything else. I am sorry to my kids' teachers for not volunteering to watch the kids at lunch, sorry to the kids for not having time to play, sorry to my boss for not writing enough stories, sorry to my friends for missing birthday dinners or jewelry parties, sorry to my parents for not spending enough time with them, and sorry to the hubby for being too tired to be a sex goddess. I am even sorry to the dogs because I don't have enough time to play ball. The list goes on and never ends. I am in a constant state of apology. Yet, the one thing I refuse to apologize for is trying to accomplish it all.

I think today's woman can have it all, but first we have to forgive ourselves and stop apologizing for trying to accomplish everything we set our minds to do. Sure, we are more than likely not going to accomplish our goals exactly as we initially planned, but that doesn't mean we need to apologize for trying, or just give up.

These days, however, I am trying to minimize my apologies and I have a new approach to the women I interact with personally or professionally. I don't want to become so calloused by the pain this world brings us that I become untouchable by anyone who I interact with. I understand everyone has their own comfort zones and not everyone is thrilled to be around someone full of enthusiasm. However, I don't want to become so protective that people view me as pretentious or out of touch.

I have been burned by other women professionally, so I can see why many women in this highly competitive field are guarded and reserved. Now, if you have read this entire book with hopes that I would throw out a few names of these women, I have to disappoint you.

However, what I can tell you is what an amazing feeling it is to receive a genuine greeting or a smile when you are sure you are going to get a condescending look or a quick brush-off . . . to truly feel as if another female knows the struggles of navigating and is willing to give you honest insight and advice so that you can avoid making a devastating mistake.

It is these women whom I admire and I aspire to be like, the women who help you gain confidence just because of a kind word or friendly gesture. Every woman is a big deal to someone. Whether that group is really big or limited to her own family doesn't really matter, because she is valuable and, without her, another person's life is affected.

Every woman is a big deal to someone. Whether that group is really big or limited to her own family doesn't really matter.

It is a hard risk to take and I am finding in some ways it is even more difficult the older I get. Shelf life for my profession is not the longest, especially for females. Men definitely have the upper hand in this realm as the more gray they show the more professional respect they are usually given. The only thing most women in broadcasting are given as they age is a chance to do infomercials or commercials for laxative yogurt or bladder-control products. This is how I know that God is definitely a man.

It's Lonely out There

I joke that I live the *Hannah Montana* type of life. The problem is, while I get the best of both worlds, it's also a very lonely world. Those at home are nice but because I don't have the time to invest in a solid friendship, I don't blame them for leaving me out of parties, lunches, or play dates. On the reverse side, because I am constantly traveling, I don't have time to really have a close friendship with anyone on the road and since most of these women are on the same schedule, neither do they. Plus, add in the element of competition and mistrust and sometimes it's just not worth opening yourself up.

It can be a very lonely life, despite what the pictures on social media might show. Most days are spent alone in a hotel room or on a flight, researching the next topic or writing the next article. Shopping is usually on my own and dining is usually in my room, wrapped in a bathrobe, prepping for the next day. Pathetic, isn't it?

No one prepared me for the loneliness, just as no one prepared me for the harsh criticisms and constant critique of the outside world. It's a catch-22: do you go out there full of sunshine, energy, and optimism and then brace yourself for the rejection, or do you stay silently in your own corner of the world and not risk getting any attention, negative or positive?

I say all of this not to put down our gender, because that would be the exact opposite of my reason for writing this book. I say all of this because I want to identify the elephant in the room. Once it's admitted and all the cards are on the table, I believe we build confidence in ourselves by knowing that we are not the only ones who have these battles. They exist in every career field. They exist in every social circle. Same drama, just different characters.

But could you imagine what the Conservative move-ment would look like if we were all honest with each other and bonded together to fight the Hillarys, the Nancys, and the Harrys of this world? The Left couldn't spew their idea of a War on Women because if anyone looks more battle weary, it's those on the Left.

My goal for writing *ROAR* is to encourage you not to shy away from these battles when they are on the Right . . . not to shy away from these battles when they are speaking honestly about conviction they feel. To light our own fireworks and know they will not be alone in the sky. It just takes one spark.

There are just some times when you have to speak your mind . . . when you're not supposed to go along with the group and when you're not supposed to just be polite and not offend. If we are willing to risk shaking up a peaceful environ-ment over subjects like clothes, relationships, and faith, then we should not be afraid to speak our mind regarding what we believe politically.

The popularity of the *Fifty Shades* series was humorous to me because I would see women going out and buying e-readers just so they could read these books without anyone ever knowing what they were actually reading. I even had one friend who took the dust cover off another book and put it on her *Fifty Shades of Grey* book just so she could read the book at the neighborhood pool.

Women looked to *Fifty Shades* for different reasons, de-pending on what stage they were in life. Young single women

liked the series because it went along with the Disney princess movies . . . except the princesses were now independent
and living in an urban city and the prince, instead of riding
in on a horse, flew on his own private jet. But the plot line
was still along the same line—a girl rescued by a handsome
prince who ends up taking her to a castle and giving her a life
of luxury and bliss.

The Cool Factor

While some women still might have blushed when they mentioned the book title, the *Fifty Shades* theme was something
that quickly took on a pop-culture cool factor—and that is
exactly what we woman should be charged with doing in the
Conservative movement. We need to unify our side . . . make
Conservatism "cool" and certain elements accessible for all
women to identify and thus bond with.

We don't have Beyoncé or the rest of the Hollywood characters who the Left brings out at campaign time to sell the idea
that not only is the Democratic party the place for women,
but it's also the only party for anyone who doesn't want to be
put in the same category as pleather, AOL, or Walkman cas-
sette players (aka old).

We need to not only make Conservatism *look* cool again,
we need to make it *be* cool. The only way to do this is an intense PR strategy which involves using the same tactics the
Left has used to get us to label our side as "lame." Let's show
that brains and beauty combined are not a bad thing and that

not only is it acceptable for women to speak a Conservative opinion but more importantly, it's encouraged. We need to stand together and demand to be included in events like *Seventeen*'s Girl Power Movement, *Glamour*'s Women of the Year, and DC's Women in Journalism party.

We also have to make sure that we don't continue to give the Left ample material to turn around and use against us. Admit it: as Conservatives, we have all seen candidates that we know from the very beginning are going to be like dynamite and not in a good way.

These candidates can be either male or female and you have to wonder if they just woke up one day and said, "I think I have nothing else to do today, so let me run for United States Congress." Or even worse, people let their egos be manipulated and join a race, not realizing they are just being used to splinter votes. This happens at both the party primary stage as well as in the general election and at every level of government.

So who should run for office and is it wrong in 2016 to play up the gender card? The dynamics are changing; in the past I would imagine most Conservative women would never want any job given to them just because they were women . . . well, unless it was as a Victoria's Secret model. Today, however, we are going to have to play the gender card. But my hope is that we do it in a way that does not insult or reduce the role of men as the Left does.

There is no checklist guaranteeing that a candidate, male or female, will win a race, but the first thing I always suggest to a person considering an office is to run against themselves and most importantly, *be honest*. Know your own weaknesses, dirty laundry, or boiling points, because I guarantee that your opponent will eventually know them and use them against you.

Also, regardless of what level of government you are running for, are you willing and able to commit the time? Running for office is a time-consuming chore. If you're not willing and able to make it more than a full-time job, you're likely just wasting what time you do commit to it. If you're currently employed, does your employer grant you any flexibility? What about your family? Would running for office put undue stress on them and limit your time with them to unacceptable levels?

These are all very important questions that have nothing to do with what you stand for or who your base might be. The last and probably the hardest question for candidates to be honest with themselves about is this: *are you the best candidate for the job?* This is a question that few potential candidates consider. To answer this you must be honest about whether or not there is another potential candidate better suited to run and to serve than you are. Is it at all possible that your running could do more harm than good to your political ideals and priorities? Is your candidacy the *best* for the party?

This is where the establishment wing and the grassroots wing (aka the Tea Party) are having the biggest divide and why the more Conservative side keeps losing on election day. Neither side can exist without the other. The establishment wing needs the passion, energy, and hard work of the Tea Party and, while it's hard for some to acknowledge, the Tea Party needs the structure and dollars of the establishment to make a difference.

The Democrats want nothing more than to see the Republican party split because not only do they win in the short term, they buy more time to secure votes for the future.

The Dollars

Then comes the issue of money, and the mighty dollar has always ruled in politics. No campaign is ever like another; however, in most cases the average you should estimate on spending is one to three dollars per voter. The easiest way to determine whether you are on the high or low end of that spectrum is to review past campaigns' financial histories as well as consider the number of candidates in the race. Obviously, if you're running against an incumbent, your cost will be more. However, realize that in some special cases, you don't need more than the incumbent . . . just the same amount.

But does the common man or woman still have a chance to win in politics? Sure, at local levels it might only take a few thousand but latest numbers show that a congressional campaign often exceeds more than $1 million per candidate with an average of $4.3 million for a Senate campaign. Once in office, some say an elected official needs to raise ten thousand dollars on average every week just to fund his or her reelection campaign.[31]

When we are talking those types of numbers, it's no wonder most folks don't run for public office, whether you are
talking about a local school-board race or a presidential campaign. Gone are the days when most people can handle a
campaign with their own paycheck. In fact, many good busi-
nessmen and women say one of the main reasons they don't
run for office is because they don't want to take the pay cut for
a state or local position while diving into their own accounts
to run for the position.

Campaign finance law is probably the subject of hundreds
of books written by law professors. However, early in 2014 I
found myself perplexed by the Supreme Court ruling in the
McCutcheon v. Federal Election Commission case. I was excited
when I first received the notice that the Supreme Court had
ruled in favor of McCutcheon. I saw Republicans getting excited and saying that political expression and freedom of speech
was being upheld by Supreme Court Justice John Roberts.

On the reverse, the Democrats immediately started acting
as though the apocalypse had happened. I was expecting to
see Senator Harry Reid on the floor of the Senate tearing his
clothes in mourning. The Daily Beast was saying this was the
end of the common man being able to run for office.

What confused me was the Democrats making it seem as
if people could now give unlimited amounts of funds to a candidate. I remembered that in the 2012 presidential election,
Democrats raised $1.07 billion and the Republicans raised
$992.5 million. I would have assumed the Supreme Court

decision would actually have helped the Democrats more, considering at this point they had the upper hand in fundraising.

Then when we look at the super-PAC donors, 49 percent of the Democratic donors gave more than a million dollars, while only 42 percent of Republican donors gave a million dollars. The majority of Republican donors were in the one hundred thousand to one million dollar range while the Democrats' majority of PAC donors were in the one million dollar range.

Despite what many say, the establishment wing of the Republican party cannot survive without the grassroots activists and the grassroots activists cannot survive without the Republican party, but that doesn't mean that I was expecting to see the grand celebrations I saw from both sides when the McCutcheon decision was announced. I want us to unite in order to repeal Obamacare, to secure our borders, and to gain back the Senate in 2014 and win the White House in 2016. I know the debate between the establishment and the Tea Party must subside in 2014 if we are going to accomplish any goals of winning the Senate; however, this showing of unity took even me by surprise.

The reason this law was so important was that it evened the playing field for our candidates, as Republicans are known for having more individual donors compared to the Democrats' unions and PAC donations. The Supreme Court decision didn't change the maximum amount a person can give to a candidate; rather it removed restrictions on the number of candidates they can give to.

This means the Koch brothers don't have to pick their favorite twenty-five to max out to . . . now, they have the right to give their money to anyone and everyone of their choice without setting a limit. Democrats, though, should be happy because the same thing goes for Democrat Savior-in-Chief George Soros.

We Are Here

Every election cycle I can remember those on the campaign trail always say this is the most important election in history. Well unfortunately this time . . . *it's true!*

Never before have we seen our country being led by so many whose intentions are to destroy all things good that America stands for.

Here is the real scary part. The more we, the Conservative females, continue to grow our voice in unity and the more our chances of taking back Congress in 2014 and the White House in 2016 increase, the more desperate the Progressives in this country will become. The more deceitfully and ambitiously they will work, and trust me, there is nothing more dangerous than those aggressive Progressives!

This is why I think the Bundy Ranch situation occurred in the spring of 2014. Now, I might have issues with the steps leading up to the Government seizure of the cattle on Clive Bundy's land. That, however, is not what I believe the real takeaway lesson was from the Bundy Ranch clash regarding grazing rights and the Bureau of Land Management.

Every American needs to ask themselves, if the federal government can come knock on the Bundy Ranch door for a reason which involves a turtle, can they knock on your door as well? Do you have elected officials at every level of government who will come to your aid?

Make no mistake; I don't believe a single honest person thinks the Bundy Ranch incident was over a protected turtle. I believe it was no coincidence that this great challenge to American freedom occurred in Harry Reid's backyard.

I can guarantee you that within the borders of Clark County (the same county where the Bundy Ranch is located and the number-one county which has elected Senate Majority Leader Harry Reid to government office since 1982), the prickly cactus has more of a voice than any rancher, much less a Conservative rancher. I cannot believe it was a coincidence that this great assault on both the First and potentially the Second Amendment occurred where Harry Reid holds the puppet strings at almost every level of government and law enforcement.

This was a test, America. This was a test by the Progressives of this country to see how much we were going to be willing to fight . . . a test to find out who was going to speak up and who was going to stay silent.

But our battle not only as patriots but also as Conservatives is just beginning because, unfortunately, those on the other side are very smart and very sneaky. They will continue to wage battles on all fronts. They will continue to do whatever they can to take away our guns, limit our speech, tear down our borders, redistribute our wealth, and whatever possible to destroy what made America the superpower of the world.

As 2016 gets closer, you are going to see a noose being tied around the necks of men. While we say there is a war on women, the real war is on the men who will be limited in their words and their actions.

Let's leave the men to fight on the front lines of war zones outside the United States because we have more then enough of a battle to fight here at home. We are not going to win if we stay divided, if we don't lock arms and honestly align ourselves together. This is where we have the most advantage over our counterparts on the Left. We know who our enemy is and we know it is our freedom and the freedom of future generations they seek to capture.

In 2005 I had the honor of going to Iraq to personally see the good work our soldiers were doing in that country. Being one of the two females in the group of predominantly male talk-show hosts, I was not prepared for seeing a country where women were truly treated as an inferior gender.

My defining *ROAR* moment came in the dirty streets of Baghdad. The soldiers were doing their daily passing out of school supplies and treats to the many packs of young school boys in the streets and the men were completely in awe of my blond curly hair that would not stay hidden underneath the armored helmet.

All of a sudden, a city bus slowly rolled by and in amazement, I watched the women climbing and fighting over each other to get to the side of the bus where I was and proudly hold out their thumbs covered in purple ink where they had just for the first time been able to vote.

At first, I was extremely scared, as I was afraid the women were going to try to throw something to hurt me, especially when all I heard were the frantic shouting voices of the women when they realized I was standing there. The Army men standing around me were also stunned. One soldier told me later they thought the women of Iraq did not like them, but realized it wasn't that they didn't like the Americans; rather, they didn't even have the freedom to show a male any attention for fear of punishment from their society.

That is what happens when we allow someone else to enslave us. Many Conservative women today are just like those ink-printed ladies in Iraq; they are just looking for a way to show the world they want freedom from the Liberal campaign that women must be Democrats.

Whether you relate more to Helen Reddy's "I am Woman, Hear Me Roar," or Katy Perry's "Roar," the point is, now is the time for you to gather your strength because it's time for us to scare off the hyenas who keep saying that the only place for a woman is in the Democratic party.

In this jungle, there is only room for one queen, and I assure you, I am going to do everything I can to make sure her name is not Hillary.

Notes

1. Philip Rucker and Scott Clement, "For 2016, Hillary Clinton Has Commanding Lead over Democrats, GOP Race Wide Open," *Washington Post*, January 30, 2014, http://www.washingtonpost.com.
2. Multiple sources, including Benjamin Shapiro, "Even Cindy Sheehan Can Go Too Far," WND Commentary, September 1, 2005, http://www.wnd.com.
3. Center for American Women and Politics, Rutgers University, *Women in the U.S. Congress 2014*, http://www.cawp.rutgers.edu; http://www.nfrw.org.
4. Ramesh Ponnuru, "How to be happy," American Enterprise Institute, December 23, 2013, http://www.aei.org.
5. Arthur C. Brooks, "Why Conservatives Are Happier Than Liberals," *New York Times Sunday Review*, July 7, 2012, http://www.nytimes.com.
6. "Couples Who Receive Government Assistance Report Less Marital Satisfaction, Commitment, Study Finds," Phys.org, September 7, 2011, http://phys.org.
7. Vicki Zakrzewski, "How to Integrate Social/Emotional Learning into Common Core," *The Blog*, The Huffington Post, April 16, 2014, http://www.huffingtonpost.com.
8. Catherine Rampell, "Median Household Income Down 7.3% Since Start of Recession," *New York Times,* March 28, 2013, http://economix.blogs.nytimes.com; Child Care Aware of America,

Parents and the High Cost of Child Care 2013 Report,
http://usa.childcareaware.org.

9. Comedy Central, "Millennials to Candidates: Humor Me," news release, October 12, 2012, http://press.cc.com.

10. Bill Flax, "The True Meaning of Separation of Church and State," *Forbes*, July 9, 2011, http://www.forbes.com.

11. Thomas Jefferson, "Query 17," in *Notes on the State of Virginia* (first published in 1785).

12. Brendan Miniter, "Bullying the Pulpits," *Wall Street Journal*, March 10, 2006, http://online.wsj.com.

13. Associated Press, "Group Protests 'Illegal' Display of Easter Crosses in Ohio Village" (April 17, 2014), http://www.foxnews.com.

14. C. S. Lewis, "The Humanitarian Theory of Punishment," in *God in the Dock : Essays on Theology and Ethics*, ed. Walter Hooper (HarperOne, 1970).

15. Kathleen O'Brien, "Obamacare religious exemption hard to get," *Washington Post*, April 28, 2014, http://www.washingtonpost.com.

16. Andrew P. Napolitano, "Obama Mocks Catholic Nuns for Resisting Obamacare Contraception Mandate," *Washington Times*, January 15, 2014, http://www.washingtontimes.com.

17. Jaime Fuller, "Here's what you need to know about the Hobby Lobby case," *Washington Post*, March 24, 2014, http://www.washingtonpost.com.

18. Statistic Brain, "Women in the Military Statistics," http://www.statisticbrain.com.

19. "How to Prepare," US Marine Corp, http://www.marines.com.

20. Office of the Secretary of Defense Sexual Assault Prevention and Response Office, *Department of Defense Fact Sheet: Secretary Hagel Issues New Initiatives to Eliminate Sexual Assault, Updates Prevention Strategy and Releases 2013 Annual Report on Sexual Assault in the Military*, http://www.sapr.mil.

21. Christina Hoff Sommers, "No, Women Don't Make Less Money Than Men," The Daily Beast, February 1, 2014, http://www.thedailybeast.com.

22. Glenn Harlan Reynolds, "Obama's war on White House women: Column," *USA Today*, April 14, 2014, http://www.usatoday.com.

23. Conrad Black, "The Gospel According to Mark Steyn," *American Spectator*, May 2014, http://spectator.org.

24. Tim Cavanaugh, "Chris Hayes Wants to Kill About 5.7 Billion People," *National Review*, April 25, 2014, http://www.nationalreview.com.

25. Hayley Dixon, "Global warming? No, actually we're cooling, claim scientists," *The Telegraph*, September 8, 2013, http://www.telegraph.co.uk.

26. Karl Rove, "The ObamaCare Debate Is Far From Over," *Wall Street Journal*, April 9, 2014, http://online.wsj.com.

27. The Heritage Foundation, "Obamacare in Pictures: Visualizing the Effects of the Patient Protection and Affordable Care Act," Spring 2014, http://www.heritage.org.

28. Guttmacher Institute, "Fact Sheet: Contraceptive Use in the United States," August 2013, http://www.guttmacher.org.

29. Ibid.

30. Jessica Goldstein, 'How MTV's '16 and Pregnant' led to declining teen birth rates," *Washington Post* Style Blog, April 9, 2014, http://www.washingtonpost.com.

31. Markkula Center for Applied Ethics, "The Power of Money: The Ethics of Campaign Finance Reform," Santa Clara University, http://www.scu.edu.

Acknowledgments

I want to thank all who have mentored me, shaped my life, and given me the adventures and stories that make up my peculiar personality.

I don't doubt that had I been born into a traditional family with traditional parents, I would be traditional. But God decided to give me Linda and Lloyd Semler. Always having an open door to anyone in need, you taught me to always be ready and willing to help, and for that I am eternally grateful.

Almost as grateful as when Chris Hughes asked for my hand in marriage thinking he was getting a somewhat spirited Southern belle. Ha! But My Love has handled this adventure together very well, remarking that God was making up for all of his days of loneliness growing up. I love you more today then I did yesterday.

Which, speaking of yesterday, in roll my in-laws, Gene and Ruth Hughes. I hope one day you can figure out exactly what I do, but in the meantime I am grateful for your always-open arms to our children in my absence and never refusing to feed my family a warm meal.

Speaking of family, I am so grateful for my sisters-in-law (yes, once a sister always a sister), Sharon Edwards and Laura Hughes, for helping me navigate the world of being a working mom, and to my brothers-in-law, Bryan Edwards, Mike Hughes, and Uncle B for never being afraid to do what it takes to keep this family going. With a family as diverse in personality as we are, no wonder Elizabeth, Hillary, Elliott, and Farrah always feel at home no matter whose house they are at.

To my Uncle Larry, Aunt Cathy, Cousin Jenny & Co, Vera, and all of my family in Anna, Illinois, I know my mother and I both have kept many of you praying over the years as you never knew what we were going to get into. Throughout the decades, though, it was always comforting to know we had a "normal" balanced side of the family.

Just as important is my newly found family. Tom, Miss Judi, and all of my Grane siblings and cousins, I hope after you read this, you will see that I inherited not only the family allergy to sulfur but also the passion and determination the Grane family is known for.

On to my friends, who still speak to me in spite of all the unreturned phone calls and missed life events (i.e., graduations, birthdays, funerals, etc.) over the past two years. I wouldn't blame you for never talking to me again, but I am really glad you still are. Melanie, Nicole, Shandra, and all of the Whappoo girls (Traci, Tiffany, Mona, Shelli, Stephanie, Victoria, Teresa, Linh) . . . since you have kept me as your friend for this long, you might as well go the rest of the distance. I guarantee God is giving an extra 10 percent in heaven to those who had to deal with me on earth.

To my mommy-life friends, I am so glad I met you as an adult, as you would have been way too cool for me in your younger years but are stuck with me because you like my husband or my kids. Just kidding. I'm thankful for the encouraging words from an angel like Mary Beth Hearn, the styling advice and humor of Jackie Mewbourne, Tracie Blaser and Jennifer Lodge's kids glow dance parties, my Jamie's DIO ladies, and the prayers and Bible studies with the ladies of my Pathfinders Sunday school class. Words cannot describe how blessed I am to have women like you constantly showing me how to be a better Christian, wife, mother, and lady.

Speaking of ladies, I would be amiss if I did not mention the groups of ladies who throughout my life have shaped me into the woman I am today. Whether it's my sisters from the Delta Mu Chapter of ZTA, the ladies of the Junior League of Nashville, the Hendersonville Woman's Club, or the Republican Women of Tennessee, all of you are fully to blame for giving me the confidence to stand up and speak. I am forever grateful for your lessons in life and relationships.

Now on to teachers: I am still grateful for all the guidance shown me by the faculty and administration of the University of Tennessee at Martin, where I knew I could always find an open door whether it be the office of the president, the deans, or my professors. I especially want to thank the amazing faculty of the communications department, particularly Teresa Collard, Dr. Robert Nanney, Dr. Richard Robinson, and the late Dorotha Norton, who was uncertain about what I would do with my communication skills but knew she didn't want to miss the show, whatever it turned out to be.

For a long time I loved broadcasting and politics, but I didn't know how much I would love working in both until

Steve Gill took a chance on a twenty-two-year-old and hired me as his executive producer. I am grateful for the experiences you let me be part of and the people you introduced me to. Despite your attempt to trade me for a camel and some gold necklaces, I would not be where I am today in media if it weren't for your mentorship. Along with Steve, I have to thank other mentors like Neil Boortz, Lars Larson, Sean Hannity, Phil Valentine, and Michael Berry for always being kind and teaching me what true talent in talk radio looks like. Finally, one of my greatest friends and mentors in talk radio and life is Rusty Humphries, who brought me out of early retirement and encouraged me to go after my goals now instead of later. With the help of Beverly Zaslow, Luke Livingston, Matthew Perdie, Liberty Alliance, and all of my former chicks with Politichicks, the tools and resources you blessed me with have allowed me to grow into the woman I am today.

Not only did Rusty introduce me to the Politichicks but also to my current boss, Todd Cefaratti, and TheTeaParty.Net team, eventually leading to the launch of the Tea Party News Network (TPNN). Todd, words cannot express the endearment I feel for you and your wife, Jennifer, for giving me the opportunity to live my dream while expressing my passion for preserving freedom and protecting this land I love. While I do my best to drive Kellen Guida, Kris Hall, Greg Campbell, Joel Frewa, Kaitlynn Lankin, Jennifer Kruse, Dan Backer, Guy Short, Alex Shively, Tim Constantine, Vandon Gene, Jennifer Burke, and Matthew Burke crazy, I know in the end we were brought together for a great purpose.

When I first signed on with TPNN, I knew I had to bring on the best PR firm to handle the fire. The team at Javelin did not know exactly what they were getting into but have handled every panicky or weepy phone call I have given them since our launch. Lauren Ehrsam and Keith Urbahn, you have done such an amazing job taking a "Tea Party Mom from the South" and turning her into the girl next door who can talk politics, pop culture, and parenthood all while keeping a smile on her face and doing media hits and speeches beyond "passable."

I mention many of my mentors throughout this book, however I cannot speak highly enough of those who have shown me kindness the past few years in the broadcast business. Charles Payne, Neil Cavuto, Stuart Varney, Tucker Carlson, Monica Crowley, Lis Wiehl, Elizabeth MacDonald, Gretchen Carlson, Elisabeth Hasselbeck, Todd Starnes, and KT McFarland never hesitated to give a kind word in passing or send an encouraging note after a great hit. While you are the top in talent, it's your humbleness and sincere attitudes I strive to always portray.

I would be remiss if I did not thank the amazing team at Worthy Publishing. I knew writing my first book was going to be an adventure, however I could not have done it without Byron, Jeana, Kyle, Morgan, Alyson, Dennis, and Mark. And thanks to Troy, Betty, Sherrie, and Julie for your efforts in selling this book to the masses.

My mother always said that it meant more to pray *after* you were finished eating to show your gratefulness. I feel like this now, as writing this book has been a spiritual journey unlike any before. Because I had to address much of my past I thought had been buried for good, coupled with physical exhaustion, writing this book made me pray a lot as I asked God for the exact words and message to give. I could not have done this without the encouragement and inspiration from pastors Don Hutchinson, Randy Goodman, and Brad

Holliman at Hendersonville First United Methodist Church. Also, considering passionate people like myself need lots of guidance, Pastor Maury Davis at Cornerstone Church always kept my evangelical light shining bright.

Last, I wrote this book for Houston and Alexandria. I am so proud of everything my mother did in her life, and I hope that one day you look back and see that in everything I did, I tried to make a better world for you. May you always know that no matter the path it takes to get where you want to go . . . you can accomplish your dreams. Chicken & Biscuit: I will always love you to the moon and back!

About the Author

Scottie Nell Hughes currently serves as the news director for the Tea Party News Network, which was launched in November 2012.

She has covered a wide variety of stories, ranging from on-the-street interview packages to entertaining yet revealing interviews with some of the most notorious names in both politics and Hollywood. Scottie's interviews have been linked on top sites like Drudge Report, Breitbart, TheBlaze, World Net Daily, and The Daily Caller, with several stories going viral. She has also appeared numerous times on *The O'Reilly Factor, Hannity, Fox and Friends, America's Newsroom, The Real Story with Gretchen Carlson, Your World with Neil Cavuto, America Live with Megyn Kelly, Varney & Co, Lou Dobbs, FBN Markets Now, Justice with Judge Jeanine, Cavuto on Business, CNN Newsroom* with Don Lemon, the former *Piers Morgan Live, CBS This Morning, Current TV, Rasmussen Reports,* as well as on the Canadian Broadcasting Company and the BBC.

Scottie also serves as a columnist for Townhall.com, TownhallFinance.com, and ChristianPost.com; she contributes to Patriot.TV and PatriotUpdate.com; and is a former PolitiChick. In addition to winning the 2012 Blog Video of the Year award by the National Bloggers Club at the 2013 Conservative Political Action Conference (CPAC), she was named by Right Wing News to their annual Top 20 Hottest Conservative Women in the New Media in 2013.

Scottie has been a part of numerous broadcasts from the Republican and Democrat National Conventions (for which she was awarded a Nashville Air Award in 2005), various national primaries, as well as the White House and the Pentagon. She also was in the first group of radio talk-show hosts sent by the Department of Defense to travel to the front-lines of Operation Enduring Freedom in Iraq and Kuwait, as well as the detention facilities at Guantanamo Bay, Cuba.

An active member in her community, Scottie was named Citizen of the Year for the City of Hendersonville, Tennessee, in 2011 as well as Member of the Year for the GFWC Woman's Club. She and her husband, Chris Hughes, have two children.

WORTHY

PUBLISHING

IF YOU ENJOYED THIS BOOK, WILL YOU CONSIDER
SHARING THE MESSAGE WITH OTHERS?

- Mention the book in a Facebook post, Twitter update, Pinterest pin, blog post, or upload a picture through Instagram.
- Recommend this book to those in your small group, book club, workplace, and classes.
- Head over to facebook.com/worthypublishing, "Like" the page, and post a comment as to what you enjoyed the most.
- Tweet "I recommend reading #ROAR by @scottienhughes // @worthypub"
- Pick up a copy for someone you know who would be challenged and encouraged by this message.
- Write a book review online.

You can subscribe to Worthy Publishing's
newsletter at worthypublishing.com.

WORTHY PUBLISHING
FACEBOOK PAGE

WORTHY PUBLISHING
WEBSITE